THE BUDDHIST TRADITION
OF
MENTAL DEVELOPMENT

The Buddhist Tradition
of
Mental Development

Peter Della Santina

Manjushri Press
Boston
2002

MANJUSHRI PRESS
P.O. BOX 391042
CAMBRIDGE, MA
02139 U.S.A.

Printed in Canada

ISBN 1-928709-03-6

10   9   8   7   6   5   4   3   2   1

Library of Congress control number 2001133130

DEDICATION

BY THE VIRTUE OF THIS WORK

MAY ALL BEINGS ATTAIN FULL ENLIGHTENMENT

Contents

INTRODUCTION

THE ORIGINS OF THE TRADITION

We call this tradition that we will be discussing the Buddhist tradition because the tradition originated with the Buddha Sakyamuni 2500 years ago in India. This is true of this particular tradition that we will study, and it is also true of other Buddhist traditions like the Theravada and Zen traditions.

This tradition comes down to us today from the Buddha Sakyamuni through a series of transmission. The first phase in this process of transmission was an oral phase. The teachings were handed down orally from master to disciple, and preserved in the memories of the disciples of the Buddha. This is called the primary oral tradition, and it continued for about four to five hundred years after the demise of the Buddha.

During this period we find the emergence of the primary literary tradition. These teachings of the Buddha began to be written down. It is still very much a codification, a crystallization of the oral tradition. We can see this from the fact that all the teachings in the primary literary tradition begin with the words "Thus, I have heard." These are believed to be the words of the Buddha's faithful attendant, Ananda, who retained the teachings in his memory, and passed them on to the other disciples at the Council that was held shortly after the demise of the Buddha.

The primary literary tradition is the canonical foundation from which further developments in the tradition proceed. Following the primary literary tradition, there was a secondary literary tradition, consisting of commentaries and explanations of the primary oral and literary traditions. Foremost among these expositors are figures like Nagarjuna who explained the doctrine of emptiness, and Asanga who focussed on the role of the mind in the production and elimination of suffering.

Contemporaneous with and subsequent to the secondary literary tradition, there was a secondary oral tradition. This had its heyday in the period from the 6th or 7th Century to about the 11th Century CE. What we have in this secondary oral tradition is the production of a very interesting group of people, the men of great attainment (Mahasiddhas). These people came from all walks of life: some from the elite and educated strata of society, some were boatmen and potters. They had one thing in common —they were particularly interested in translating or expressing the wisdom embodied in the primary and secondary literary traditions in terms of ordinary daily life. They used all kinds of symbols and events that we find in our daily life to translate the abstract philosophy of the literary traditions into immediate living experiences.

These three traditions (primary literary, secondary literary, and secondary oral) which, on the one hand, are academic and abstract, and, on the other hand, experiential and living, were transmitted to Tibet from the 7th to the 12th Century. Thus, a remarkable mirror image of the apex of Buddhism was preserved in Tibet. When Buddhism declined, and was almost eradicated in India as an identifiable independent tradition, it was preserved in Tibet. It was preserved in Tibet through a continuous process of renewal and re-verification, through the application of the teachings in the context of personal experience. The teachings were preserved not only as cultural or intellectual fossils, but also as a living tradition—re-experimented and re-experienced by its practitioners. This is the tradition that we will be discussing here.

The Key to Self Development

We also call this a tradition of mental development because in Buddhism the mind is the key to development. It is the most essential thing in personal development. Different traditions begin at different points. For example, in the Semitic traditions, one begins with God. In certain political philosophies like Marxism, one begins with society or the economic sphere. In Buddhism, we begin with mind. Mind is the key to progress. Why is this so? It is because there is no experience without mind. There is no happiness and no frustration without mind. All of these are mind-dependent. All our experiences come to us through our mind. The sense organs—eyes, ears, nose, tongue and skin—do not sense apart from the mind. Thus, it is clear that if we want to change the character of our experience, we must change the character of our mind. If we wish to cover the entire surface of the earth with carpet in order to protect our bare feet from the sticks and stones, it would be a very difficult task. But simply by covering our feet with leather, it is as if the whole surface of the earth were covered with leather. In the same way, if we want to remove greed, anger and delusion from the earth, it would be a very difficult task. But by removing greed, anger and delusion from our mind, it is as if they were removed from the world. This is why we have this focus on mind as the key to self-development. By changing the condition and character of our mind, we can change the character of our experience.

One of the very first steps in mental development is observation of the behavior of our minds. We will see that almost exclusively our minds are reactive. In other words, our minds continuously react to stimuli. When we see certain images, our minds react to them. When we hear certain sounds, taste certain foods, smell certain scents, our minds react to them. There is almost no occasion in the course of an undeveloped mental continuum when our minds are not reactive. A well-known teacher says that our minds are like vending machines. You put in a coin and you get a reaction.

This reactive process of the mind is only a semi-conscious process. We are not fully aware. We are sleepwalking, so to speak. We are constantly reacting in a mechanical automatic way. We are cogs in a machine because we have no self-awareness. But once we become aware of the reactive character of the mind, of how much we are prisoners to reactions, this is the beginning of mental development. This awareness creates a modicum of space in which to begin a new kind of mental process - in which to shift over from reaction to creativity.

In this way, we can begin to work with the mind, enlarging that area of awareness, control and development so that eventually we are acting in a free, creative and positive way. We cease to be cogs in a machine. We can exert a positive influence both in our personal life and in the lives of others. We will be talking about mental development—about how we can use the power of this most powerful thing we have at our disposal, the power of our mind, to transform the quality of our experience.

1. CONFIDENCE AND DEVELOPMENT

The tradition with which we are dealing is concerned with the alleviation of suffering and the enhancement of happiness that are experienced by conscious beings. In this context, it has been said right at the outset that one ought to approach the study of this tradition with a particular kind of attitude in that one ought to study the tradition with a view to benefiting oneself and others. And one ought not to take up the study of the tradition to gain power over others, in order to enhance one's own ego, or to become a very erudite person, well versed in esoteric subjects, able to impress others. The motivation for taking up these studies ought to be a genuine desire to eradicate suffering and to enhance happiness for oneself and others.

What do we mean by mental development? By mental development we do not mean only those brief periods of our lives which we spend sitting cross-legged, counting our breath or looking at an image or reciting a formula. By mental development, we mean all those techniques or methods whereby we can change our mental orientation whereby we can change the way in which we view ourselves and the world around us. In this tradition, we are concerned with indicating the integration, the union between meditation, and our daily ordinary experience. In a sense, we are going to try to make our daily experience part of our meditation, and we are going to try to make our meditation part of our daily experience. We will try to show

how we can develop our mind in order to improve and transform the nature and quality of our life within the framework of the Buddhist tradition.

ATTITUDES TOWARDS THE TEACHINGS

There are certain specific attitudes that one ought to cultivate in one's approach towards the teachings. It is not that cultivating these attitudes is beneficial for the teaching. Rather, it is that the cultivation of these attitudes will help in getting the most out of the teachings. We can describe the correct attitude towards the teachings by means of the analogy of a vessel. We liken the person who approaches the teachings to a vessel, and we liken the teachings to a liquid that is to be poured into the vessel. When we pour liquid into a vessel, we need to avoid three situations. The first situation is when the vessel is upside-down. This situation is similar to the situation of those who listen to the teachings with a closed mind and are not receptive. They are not willing to allow the teachings to penetrate their mind, to enter their experience. The second situation is when the vessel has a hole in the bottom. This represents the proverbial case of what we hear going in one ear and coming out of the other ear. Those who approach the teachings must avoid the fault of letting the teachings slip away from them. They must cultivate retentive ability, so that they can remember the teachings. The third situation is when the vessel has impurities in it. For example, if we pour fresh milk into a vessel that has a residue of spoiled milk, this will spoil the fresh milk. If the listener has impurities in his mind - as for example if he is listening to the teachings because of egotistical or selfish motives - the teachings will be soured by those impurities and he will not be getting the full effect of the teachings. When we approach this tradition, we need to cultivate receptivity, retentiveness, and have an uncontaminated mind.

We can also describe the attitudes to be adopted towards the teachings by means of a therapeutic analogy. This means that the teachings will be most effective if we regard the teacher, as for example the Buddha, as a physician. The Buddha was known as the king of physicians because his intention was to free sentient beings from the illness of suffering. One regards the teachings as one would regard the medicine. One regards oneself as the patient. One regards one's own afflictions, one's own negative egotistical emotions—greed, anger and delusion—as the illness. Finally, one regards the practice as the treatment as the therapy. If one adopts these attitudes towards the teachings, then the teachings will be most effective. These attitudes have been encouraged over the long history of this tradition because they have proven to be efficacious in deriving the greatest benefit from the tradition.

IMPORTANCE OF CONFIDENCE

The essential prerequisite for mental development within the Buddhist tradition is confidence or faith. We find this term appearing frequently in all the Buddhist traditions, whether we are talking about the literary tradition (primary or secondary) or the oral tradition. Confidence or faith is a prerequisite or forerunner to subsequent practices. For example, in the Abhidharmakosha, a compendium of higher teaching composed by Vasubandhu, we find the following factors mentioned as important for progress towards freedom and emancipation. The first of them is confidence and that is followed by compassion, diligence,

Buddha King of Psysicians

wisdom and wholesome conduct. Again, in the seven holy treasures, which were first transmitted by the Buddha to his son Rahula, confidence heads the list.

Faith also heads the list of the five spiritual faculties, the faculties that lead to progress along the path to freedom —faith, energy or endeavor, mindfulness or awareness, concentration and wisdom. In all these cases we find confidence or faith as being important in mental development.

We also find a number of similes used to illustrate the importance of confidence or faith. It is said that confidence is like a seed because it precedes the sprout of mental development. Confidence is like a mother because it gives birth to the offspring of spiritual development. Confidence is like a symbol because it safeguards and preserves a kind of representation of the goal that is to be achieved. Again, it is said that confidence is like a treasure because one can draw upon it in the same way that one can draw upon one's material resources. In the context of mental development, one can draw upon one's store of confidence in order to achieve one's goals. It is also said that confidence is like our hands and feet–because with the help of our hands and feet we can climb the ladder of mental development that leads to happiness and freedom.

DEFINITION OF CONFIDENCE

Let us define confidence or faith a little bit more precisely in the context of the Buddhist tradition. When we speak of confidence or faith we do not mean "blind faith" or an absolute or rigid adherence to any set of absolute doctrines. What we mean here is a positive, constructive attitude of mind. What we mean is confidence or belief in the possibility of success. It is in this sense that faith or confidence is a prerequisite to any progress on the path to personal emancipation. If we do not believe in the possibility of success, then all our endeavors will be fruitless and ineffective. For example, if we do not believe that we can learn how to swim, it will not avail us to take lessons in swimming because we lack that initial confidence in the possibility of success—not necessarily in terms of the certainty of success but in terms of the possibility of success. We can see this also illustrated in the attitude of an experimental scientist who has an initial confidence in a working hypothesis. If he did not have confidence in that hypothesis, then he would never invest the time, effort and materials required to carry out the experiment to verify the hypothesis. Thus, in the Buddhist tradition, we speak of confidence in the working hypothesis, in the possibility of mental development, and in the path to liberation. If we do not believe in the possibility of improving the nature and quality of our experience, of making it better, then there is no use in attending classes, in studying yoga, etc.

STAGES OF CONFIDENCE

In Buddhism, there are three stages of confidence or faith. The first is termed clear or limpid confidence or faith. This means that we have a clear perception of the desirability of alleviating suffering and frustration, the desirability of a transformed mode of experience. This is followed by a stage which we call aspiring confidence or faith. Having seen clearly the desirability of the goal, we now cultivate an aspiration to achieve this transformed state of mental development for ourselves.

The third stage in the development of faith or confidence is called confident faith, or believing faith, or certain faith. This means that as we progress along the path of mental development, as we implement the methods and techniques of mental development, we begin to transform that limpid confidence, and that aspiration to achieve that goal for ourselves into our own experience, so that our faith becomes definite, it becomes not something distant that we seek from afar and strive for but something close at hand.

OBJECTS OF CONFIDENCE

1 Law of Karma

At this stage you may ask, "Confidence or faith in what?" We are talking about working hypotheses. The first working hypothesis in which we need to have confidence in if we are to reap the benefits of this Buddhist tradition of mental development is the hypothesis which affirms in the moral sphere - the law of action and reaction, the law of cause and effect. We have Newton's law of action and reaction in the physical sphere. In the moral sphere we also have a law of action and reaction, the law of karma. In other words, wholesome actions bring about good results, while unwholesome actions bring about bad results.

2 Four Noble Truths

The second working hypothesis that we need to have confidence in is the Four Noble Truths. These are the Truth of suffering, the Truth of the cause of suffering, the Truth of the end of suffering, and the Truth of the path or method which leads to the end of suffering. The *First Noble Truth* is a matter for all of us to observe in our everyday lives. We are all subject to suffering and frustration.

The *Second Noble Truth* is the truth of the cause of suffering—ignorance, craving and ill will. In finding the solution to a problem, we need first to look for its cause. If your lights go out, you will want to find out the cause: whether the fuse has blown or whether it is a power failure. Ignorance is the belief in an ego, a self that is separate from and opposed to everything that surrounds us. So long as I believe in a self as separate from and opposed to the world and people around me, so long as I have this basic ignorance, this fundamental duality, then I will constantly be in a state of frustration and tension. This is because I will want those things that support and benefit my self, and I will be opposed to and be adverse to those things that threaten my self. Here we have the basic triad of emotional or psychological instability—ignorance which is the bifurcation into self and other, and based upon this bifurcation we have greed and ill will.

The *Third Noble Truth* is the Truth of the end of suffering. When we eliminate the causes of suffering we eliminate this basic emotional instability. We find ourselves in a situation characterized by the end of suffering, the experience of emancipation.

The *Fourth Noble Truth* is the Truth of the path. It supplies the methods, the therapy by means of which we are to eliminate the causes of suffering.

We can draw parallels between the Four Noble Truths and the scientific steps of observation (identification of a problem), theory and hypothesis formulation, experiment, and verification. As in science, the Four Noble Truths are a working hypothesis. The object of the exercise is to put the techniques of the path into practice, and see whether they lead to the elimination of the causes of the problem.

3 Triple Gem

The third hypothesis in which we need to have initial confidence is the efficacy of the Triple Gem - the *Buddha* (the Enlightened One), the *Dharma* (the teachings), and the *Sangha* (the community of emancipated or developed individuals). Confidence in the Buddha, Dharma and Sangha is important because, firstly, with regard to the Buddha, one needs to have confidence in the possibility of achieving emancipation. The Buddha is a symbol of the achievement of that emancipation. Having confidence in the Buddha means having confidence in the possibility of achieving enlightenment. Confidence in the Dharma means a willingness to experiment with it, a willingness to put it into practice to see if it works. The Buddha said, "Put my teachings into practice. If they work, use them, if they do not work, discard them." But in order to put Dharma into practice, there has to be an open-mindedness, a confidence in those teachings. Finally, confidence in the Sangha. We are all separated by many centuries and by many hundreds of miles from the time and place in which the Buddha taught. What connects us to the teachings of the Buddha, what completes the circuit, is the Buddhist community, the community of developed individuals who have experimented with the teachings, practiced the teachings, and who are now in a position to assist us.

To summarize, the working hypotheses in which we need to develop initial confidence are the Law of Karma, the Four Noble Truths, and the Triple Gem.

Having done this, we now achieve unshakable confidence or faith. This is confidence that is not affected by greed, anger, ignorance and fear. The first three are the basic psychological or negative emotional influences.

When we have attained unshakable faith, we will not abandon our confidence in these working hypotheses because of greed, anger or ignorance. We will not be tempted away from our commitment to mental development by, for example, the wish to earn a great deal of money, or because of anger towards another individual, or fear of blame. Unshakable confidence or faith is cultivated through the consideration and the recollection of the desirability of the goal and through gradual implementation of the methods so that we draw closer towards that goal.

IMPORTANCE OF TAKING REFUGE

Let us now look at the first practical step on the path to happiness and freedom in the Buddhist tradition of mental development. This first practical step is the taking of refuge. What is the importance of taking refuge? Any endeavor whose object is the radical transformation of experience is bound to be a long and arduous process. If someone suffering from an illness is going to undertake a long course of treatment, he needs something to place his confidence in, something to sustain him. In the context of mental development, at the moment there is a vast gulf between ourselves and the emancipated state of liberation. It is going to take a lot of effort and time. There are going to be difficulties in implementing the methods. No journey that is undertaken is without obstacles. It is the institution of refuge that will support us in the journey of mental development. In Buddhism, one takes refuge in the Triple Gem in order that they may help us along the path to liberation.

CAUSES OF TAKING REFUGE

There are three motivations for taking refuge. These motivations are stratified in the sense that the first is the most limited and is of the smallest scope and intention. The second is of medium scope and intention, while the last is of the greatest scope and intention. The first motivation is fear or anxiety. This is analogous to the feeling that many of us share in the sense that we are all anxious about forces beyond our control, about the possibility of unwanted accidents befalling us, about the experiences of illness and death, and we seek some way to protect ourselves from these unwanted eventualities. This fear or anxiety is also central to the growth and evolution of primitive religions. Sometimes it is said that religions grow out of fear. To a degree this is true, but one can also say that science grows out of fear as it grows out of the desire to guard against unwanted circumstances. This is the first kind of motivation. It is the most negative and the most selfish.

The second motivation is confidence or faith. This is more positive than the first in the sense that the action is not motivated by fear. It means that having seen the qualities of the Buddha, his teachings, and the community, one develops confidence in their excellence. One is then motivated to take refuge in them because one sees them as something valuable.

The highest and broadest in scope of the three motivations is the motivation of compassion. This means that one goes for refuge not only to achieve security and positive development for oneself, but also for other living beings as well. This is like a person who seeks shelter when caught in a storm. His first impulse is to seek shelter for himself. This is illustrative of the motivation of fear. Next, he will seek out a shelter which promises a secure protection from the storm. In other words, he would not take shelter under a tree but in a sturdy building. This is illustrative of taking refuge out of confidence, because one understands the quality of the objects of refuge. Finally, having decided upon that place of refuge, he turns his vision outward, and calls to his other fellow pedestrians to take refuge in the secure place. This is illustrative of the motivation of compassion.

OBJECTS OF REFUGE

When we take refuge in the Triple Gem, we take refuge first of all in the Buddha in his two-fold aspect. The Buddha has two dimensions or aspects. One aspect is his transcendental dimension. This dimension is inexpressible, beyond thought and words. In addition to this transcendental dimension, the Buddha also has a phenomenal or form dimension which appears in the world. When we take refuge in the Buddha, we must understand him in his two-fold aspect. This can also be expressed in terms of freedom from and freedom to. In this sense, the Buddha's transcendental aspect is an expression of his freedom from. It is through his attainment of this state that he is free from the bondage of birth and death. However, he is also free to appear in the world in order to help other sentient beings to achieve this two-fold freedom.

We take refuge in the Dharma, in the sense of the teachings, as it is embodied in the literature of the Buddhist tradition and in the sense as it is realized and experienced by ourselves. Thus, the Dharma has two aspects. It has an external, intellectual aspect—an aspect in words and letters. It also has an internal, experiential aspect—an aspect which is known and proved through realization.

Finally, we take refuge in the community of emancipated, enlightened beings.

HOW TO TAKE REFUGE

What is the manner in which we take refuge? First of all, let us return to the analogy of a journey. To achieve the total transformation of our experience is a long process. It is like traveling to a distant city. If we were to travel to a distant city, we will want a guide, a path or a vehicle, and traveling companions. The Triple Gem fulfills these requirements. The Buddha is like a guide who leads us to our goal, having made the journey himself, being familiar with the way. Thus, the way in which we regard the Buddha when taking refuge is to regard him as a guide. We look upon the Dharma as a path, as a vehicle. It is not an accident that the various Buddhist teachings are called vehicles (yanas). The Sangha are our traveling companions, so that when we make the journey, we do not have to travel alone. We have someone to share our experience.

THE THREE STAGES OF PRACTICE

1 Preparatory Practice

More specifically, we take refuge by means of a three-step process. The three stages are the preparatory stage, the actual practice, and the concluding or dedicatory stage. In the case of other meditative practices, the taking of refuge itself will be the preparatory stage, and the other meditations will be the actual practice. But here, because we are concerned with the taking of refuge, the refuge taking will be the actual practice. The preparatory stage is the preparation of suitable conditions for the taking of refuge. This entails tidying up the place in which one is going to take refuge. This is important because it acts as an external symbol of mental purification, of mental ordering. In fact, for those of you who spend a portion of your time washing the dishes, or cleaning the house, this is an excellent meditative practice because it is a symbol of clearing of the mind of the clutter of those reactive habits. After tidying up, we might go even further and light incense, etc., all of which create a peaceful, ordered environment.

2 *Actual Practice*

The actual taking of refuge involves sitting before an image of the Buddha. One will be sitting in the lotus or half-lotus posture. The image of the Buddha should be at about eye-level, so that one can easily focus one's eyes on it. It should be at a distance of about five feet. It should be easily seen (not in shadow), and it should be firm and steady (it should not shake or tremble because of drafts, etc.). One sits in this way, with one's back straight, with one's neck slightly bent, with one's eyes focussed on the image, with one's mouth slightly open, and with the tongue curled slightly upward. One has one's hands either resting on one's lap with the fingers intertwined and with the thumbs touching, or one can rest the palms on the knees, again with the index fingers and thumbs touching. Sitting in this way, one recites the formula of refuge.

The formula of refuge runs as follows:

"In Buddha. Dharma and Sangha, I take refuge until enlightenment is reached."

Here, we have an indication of the particular orientation of the Mahayana tradition, the goal of which is the achievement of Buddhahood of the two-fold freedom. In the second half of the formula, one goes on to say:

"By the merit of the practice of generosity and other wholesome actions, may I attain Buddhahood for the sake of all living beings."

The reference to generosity and other positive actions is a reference to the Bodhisattva Path, the path of the six perfections which we will look more closely at in a later chapter.

3 Concluding Practice

The actual practice is followed by the concluding, or dedicatory practice. This is a kind of focussing of the energy created by the actual practice. It has been said that dedication is like the placing of a lampshade on an electric bulb. With a naked electric bulb, the light is diffuse. It issues forth in all directions. With a lampshade, the light rays become focussed in one direction. In the same way, we have created some positive energy through our practice of this meditation. Having created this energy, we need to channel it so that it will not spread out in all directions in a diffuse way. By an active conscious intention, we want to direct it to a particular goal. We do this by means of the dedicatory concluding practice. Here we say:

"By this merit may I attain Buddhahood and may all beings without exception also attain Buddhahood."

With the dedicatory concluding practice, we focus the positive energy created through the practice of refuge on the goal of Buddhahood for the sake of all sentient beings.

Benefits of Taking Refuge

The taking of refuge has a number of important benefits. In general terms, we have already indicated that the taking of refuge is a support, an aid, a framework, something which sustains us over the course of the path towards liberation. In addition, the taking of refuge has inconceivable and immense benefits insofar as it is the first step in a process where the eventual result is achievement of Buddhahood. This is why it is said that if the benefit of taking refuge had a form, if it were material, the universe would not be sufficiently large to contain it.

Commitments

Finally, the taking of refuge implies a certain commitment. This commitment is a special orientation towards the Triple Gem, and the things for which it stands. Taking of refuge in the Buddha does not mean that one cannot continue to revere other religious figures, other embodiments of religious excellence, other gods, or other holy teachers. But what it does mean is that, as one's spiritual guide in the practice of this path, the Buddha is recognized as being paramount, as having an exclusive place in this endeavor to achieve mental development. This only makes good sense. One would not be going to one doctor and also listening to the advice of another doctor. You have to choose your doctor if you are to carry out a consistent program of therapy. You may decide to change your doctor, but so long as you are following a particular course of therapy it makes sense to place a particular doctor in a special position. This is the first kind of commitment implied in the taking of refuge.

Secondly, with respect to the Dharma. The essential part of the commitment in the context of the teachings is the endeavor to observe the principle or practice of non-injury, to avoid harming others. This is the very foundation of Buddhist morality and it is the most basic commitment in regard to the teachings.

In regard to the Sangha, the commitment implies the cultivation of those associates who share this non-violent orientation. One might talk about this in terms of cultivating a community of Buddhists but that would be to miss the point. It is not so important whether one is called a Buddhist but whether one lives according to Buddhist principles. Thus, the commitment to the Sangha is to cultivate those friends who also share a commitment to non-injury.

II. Opportunity and Transcience

The purpose of considering the topics of opportunity and transience is to motivate one to make efforts to achieve the goal of enlightenment. In general, opportunity and transience have a dual or complementary function. Opportunity is the recognition of the chance which we have to achieve self-transformation and enlightenment. Recognition of transience is a spur to strive for that transformation and enlightenment without delay because of the transitory nature of this opportunity.

Precious Human Form

In this Buddhist tradition of mental development, the first thing for us to consider is the precious nature of the human condition. Some may consider this as somewhat unusual as normally one thinks of the Buddhist tradition as one which emphasizes suffering. Despite the fact that suffering is an undeniable fact of life, and that the sufferings of old age, disease, death, separation, frustration, etc. are undeniably a part of the human condition, yet here we talk about the precious nature of the human condition. This is recognition of the fact that the human condition is the most potentially beneficial. The potential embodied in the human form is no less than the highest potential of conscious existence which is enlightenment. So the first step in the consideration of the nature of opportunity is the recognition of the precious nature of the human form, the recognition that the only worthy purpose of human existence is self-transformation. It is often asked, what is it that distinguishes the human being from an animal? If we think about this for a little while, we can identify precious little that distinguishes the human from an animal, if we do not consider religious consciousness and perhaps aesthetic and artistic consciousness. These kinds of consciousness distinguish humanity from the animals. It is often said that in eating, sleeping and copulating, etc. there is nothing that distinguishes man from the animal. It is only in so far as he strives for self-transformation that a human being is distinguished from the lower forms of conscious existence. The worthy purpose of the human form is self-transformation to achieve freedom and this purpose can be achieved from the human condition.

DIFFICULTY OF OBTAINING HUMAN BIRTH

1 Cause

Recognizing the precious and unique character of the human condition also implies recognizing the rarity of the human condition - the difficulty of obtaining human birth. This is traditionally considered from four points of view. First, the difficulty of obtaining human birth is considered from the point of view of cause. The primary causes for achieving human birth are wholesome actions - actions which are not motivated by greed, anger or delusion. If we examine our conduct and that of others, we can see that the number of actions which are free from the taints of greed, anger and delusion are relatively few. Thus, in so far as wholesome actions are relatively rare, human birth is difficult to obtain from the point of view of the rarity of its cause.

2 *Number*

Second, human birth is difficult to obtain from the point of view of number. What this means is that if we calculate the total number of sentient beings, human beings (although there are more than four billion) are relatively few. The equation is even more lopsided in the context of the Buddhist tradition when we take into account the other realms of existence (realms of hell-beings, hungry ghosts, animals, demi-gods and gods). But even if we leave the other realms out and simply compare the number of human beings with the number of animals, non-human beings predominate. Thus, from the point of view of number, the human condition is a rarity.

3 *Illustration*

The third of the four ways in which we consider the difficulty of achieving the human form is illustrated by a number of examples. One of the examples used by the Buddha is the example of a blind tortoise dwelling at the bottom of an ocean and a yoke being tossed about on the surface of the ocean by the wind and waves. If the tortoise comes to the surface of the ocean once in a hundred years, the chances of that tortoise placing its head through the opening in that yoke are similar to the chances of achieving human birth rather than birth in another realm. It is also said that just as if one were to throw a handful of peas against a stone wall, the chances of one of those peas sticking in a crack in the wall would be small, so the chances of achieving human birth are similar.

4 *Nature of Human Birth*

The fourth way of considering the difficulty of achieving

human birth is in terms of the nature of human birth. This is where we begin to recognize differentiation in the particular nature or qualities of diverse human births. It is not sufficient just to be born as a human being in order to enjoy the full potential or opportunity that the human form brings with it. For example, had we been born in an Ethiopian village, although being born as a human being, we would not have the full opportunity for the development and transformation of experience that human birth can offer.

To summarize, by considering in these four ways—in terms of cause, number, example and the particular nature of certain human conditions—we consider the difficulty and the rarity of obtaining a human form. Here, we can begin to see the intention behind these considerations. Many of us, despite our relatively fortunate circumstances, go about complaining about our difficulties. Yet in comparison to the other forms of existence, even to many other human beings, we have untold opportunities for positive development, for transforming the nature of our experience, and for influencing the nature of the experience of others.

EIGHT FREEDOMS

There is an elaboration of this idea of the rarity and the precious character of the human form in the Buddhist tradition. This is usually spoken of in terms of the eighteen opportune conditions, or the eight freedoms and the ten positive conditions. They are referred to as the happy coincidence in some texts. In order to understand the eight freedoms, we need to understand the existence of the other realms in the Buddhist tradition. The first four of the eight freedoms refer to freedom from birth in one of these other realms—the realm of the hell beings, the hungry ghosts, the animals and the demi-gods and gods. In Buddhism, rebirth among the gods is not to be desired because the gods are distracted by their pleasures, and they find it difficult to devote themselves through self-development. They do not have that goad of frustration and anxiety, that feeling that something is not quite right that induces one to try to make it better. The fifth freedom is freedom from birth among unlearned people, among communities who have no access to education and the techniques of self-development. The sixth is birth among people who are inimical to and who reject the practice of self-development. The seventh is freedom from having committed unwholesome actions of very great weight. These include patricide and matricide. The negative energy of such actions is said to obstruct the opportune situation of pursuing the path of enlightenment. The eighth freedom is freedom from having been born in a situation where one's senses are defective. This has to be understood primarily in terms of what in Buddhism is the sixth sense—the mind that senses ideas. Here we are primarily concerned with mental defects. If the mind's ability to understand ideas is impaired, obviously this will be an impediment to following the path of self-development.

TEN ENDOWMENTS

Alongside these eight freedoms, there are also ten positive circumstances or ten endowments. These are divided into two groups. The first five are internal; they have to do with the individual's own qualities. The second five are external; they have to do with an individual's environment or his circumstances. The first five are parallel to, or complementary to, a number of freedoms that we considered previously.

Firstly, one must be born as a human being. Secondly,

one has to be born in a "central" realm. This means a realm where one has access to education and to the techniques of self-development. Thirdly, one must have sound senses, be of sound mind. Fourthly, one must have confidence or faith, a positive attitude towards the process of self-development. Fifthly, one must have accumulated the positive potential which is attained through the performance of wholesome actions. These are the five internal positive circumstances. The five external circumstances are, firstly, birth at the right time. This means that one has to be born in an era when an enlightened being has appeared. Secondly, one must be born at a time when the methods of self-transformation have been taught. In other words, not only should there have to have been a Buddha, but he has to have taught the methods of self-development. Thirdly, these teachings must continue to exist. Had his teachings not survived to our time, then this would not be a positive endowment. Fourthly, there must be followers of the path to self-transformation in order to assist in our pursuit of the teachings. Lastly, there must be support for one's efforts. This can take the form of moral support, psychological support, or it can take the form of material support, like the existence of monasteries, temples, schools, etc.

In summary, these are the eight freedoms and the ten endowments which together make up the full complement of the happy coincidence. If we consider the rarity of this complement of negative and positive conditions conducive to the endeavor of self-development, we will recognize that it is extremely rare to have this unique opportunity. In fact, it is said whoever uses the human form wrongly, whoever fails to use this opportunity for self-transformation and achieving enlightenment, such a person is as foolish as one who uses a jeweled vase for spittle. It is also said that the human form is like a wish-fulfilling gem because if rightly used, the human form can result in the achievement of any goal right up to the achievement of enlightenment. If one fails to use the opportune conditions for the purpose of self-transformation and making progress towards enlightenment, one is throwing away an opportunity which one does not know when one will get again.

The purpose of considering the precious human form and the difficulty of obtaining it together with the opportune conditions is to encourage one to practice self-development, to practice the Dharma. Having this remarkable opportunity, one ought not to waste it.

But recognizing that we have this precious human form and these opportune conditions is not enough. We must also recognize the transience, the impermanence of this opportunity. In order to understand the full implications of having this opportunity, we must consider the fact of transience, impermanence or change. Impermanence is one of the cardinal doctrines of Buddhism. It is the first of the three universal characteristics of reality (impermanence, suffering and not-self). Of course Buddhism is not alone in having recognized the importance and significance of impermanence. The most famous early thinker in the Greek tradition to recognize the importance and significance of impermanence was Heroclitus, who said. "You cannot step into the same river twice."

In the Buddhist tradition, it is said that the universe consists of three planes of existence (dhatus). The first of these is the realm of sense desire—the realm in which sentient beings are controlled by sense desire. This realm includes the lower realms—the realms of animals and human beings, as well as the realms of some of the gods.

3 dhatus
desire
form
formless

23

Above the realm of sense desire, there is the realm of form. Here we have beings whose existence is material but who are not subject to sense desire. Above the realm of form, we have the formless realm of immaterial, spiritual beings. All these realms of the universe are impermanent and transient, like clouds. Birth and death, it is said, are like the movements of dancers in a dance. Life itself is like a flash of lightning or a waterfall. These are some of the similes used in the perfection of wisdom literature (Prajnaparamita) to describe impermanence. Everything around us is changing very rapidly, every moment. Every instant, things change. Nothing remains the same even for a moment. We are all different now from the way that we were earlier this evening; even different from the way we were a moment ago. This has been largely substantiated by science. Most of the cells of our body are replaced over varying periods of time. Even those cells which are not replaced, like nerve cells, undergo constant changes in the elements within the cells. Even with regard to the body there is a constant process of change as is the case with the physical universe.

IMPERMANENCE

In the Buddhist tradition, a very special point is made of the fact that remembering impermanence and change is an effective teaching device. It is said that the recollection of, and the understanding of, impermanence is a most excellent teacher: that it is second only to the recollection of, and understanding of the ultimate truth. Recollecting impermanence is an antidote to desire and to suffering. It is also a key to understanding the ultimate truth. It is a spur to practice, to endeavor.

How is this so? Understanding impermanence is an

antidote to desire. How many of our desires and enmities pale into insignificance if we remember impermanence, if we remember that situations change every moment, every day, every month, every year of our lives. Remembering impermanence is an antidote to suffering because even unhappy situations can be borne more easily if we remember that, like happiness, unhappy situations are impermanent. It will not go on forever. Remembering impermanence is a spur, is an additional incentive to practice the Dharma. This is because if we remember impermanence, that life and death follow each other as rapidly as the movements of dancers in a dance, then we will recognize that this human form with the opportune conditions is impermanent. It can vanish at any moment. Finally, remembering impermanence is an intimation of the ultimate truth. This is because the ultimate truth, the way things are in actuality, is a development from an extension of impermanence.

Impermanence implies the insubstantiality of the personality and the insubstantiality of phenomena. What do we mean by this? In a situation in which our personality, that which we call ourselves is constantly changing, we cannot speak in terms of a permanent, identical individual. This is the Buddhist doctrine of not-self (anatma). This doctrine of not-self does not reject continuity. It does not reject the notion that there is a relationship that exists between diverse moments of the developmental process of the personality. There is a continuity between what we were an hour ago, or a year ago, and what we are now, but there is not any identity. This lack of identity is a logical consequence of impermanence. If the factors that make up the personality—matter, feeling, perception, volition and mind are constantly changing, if they do not remain the same for a moment, then there is no room for any independent, permanent, unchanging self. It is in this way that the Buddhist teaching of not-self is derived from an understanding of impermanence.

Just as the teaching of the insubstantiality of the personality is derived from impermanence, the teaching of the insubstantiality of phenomena is also derived from impermanence. This is because in a situation characterized by constant change, we cannot speak of an identical, permanent phenomenon.

The recognition of the insubstantiality of the personality and phenomena together imply what in Buddhism is called emptiness (Shunyata). The word Shunyata itself invites certain misinterpretations. Emptiness may suggest a void, nothingness, something which is not. But emptiness is not exactly this. Shunyata does not only mean emptiness; it also means fullness, like the fullness of a balloon. It means being swollen, pregnant. This emptiness is not nothingness. Rather it is indeterminacy, fluidity, dynamism, relativity. In other words, it is indeterminate, infinite potentiality. It is the absence of any fixed, static nature. It is this emptiness which provides that openness in which self-development and self-transformation can take place. It is the emptiness which allows for the possibility of creativity, of transforming our own experience and that of others from one characterized by suffering to one characterized by freedom. This is because in a situation in which persons and things have their own fixed nature, nothing could ever change. No ignorant human being could become educated. There would not be movement nor growth. It is this emptiness which provides the potentiality for growth. This is also true when we speak of phenomena because how we take phenomena is crucial to our progress on the path. If we take phenomena in a certain way, then they will impede our progress, if we take phenomena in another way, they will enhance our progress. So it is not what phenomena are in themselves because in themselves they are empty. It is how we take phenomena that is important. There is a saying by a little known French existentialist who wrote in the 1940's "A knife is neither true nor false. But one who grasps it by the blade is surely in error." This is how phenomena, objects are. They are neither good nor bad in themselves, they are empty. They have no identity. They have no character of their own. It is how we take them. If we take them in a certain way, we progress towards self-transformation. If we take them in another way, we get hurt. We create more suffering for ourselves.

Thus, understanding impermanence is very important. If we understand impermanence, we will understand the insubstantiality of personality and phenomena. We will understand emptiness. We will understand this dynamic, open, infinitely potent nature of reality. Shunyata also means zero. Thus, zero is nothing in itself, yet without it we would not have 10, 100, etc. It should also be pointed out that these ideas are not only important in a metaphysical and transcendental sense. They are ideas that have a very real application in our lives. No one can succeed in their profession or personal life without some kind of understanding of impermanence and insubstantiality. If we do not understand impermanence, we will not change with the times; we will not be able to adapt, to cope with new technology, new situations. If we do not understand the insubstantiality of personality, we will make the mistake of believing that the people around us, our friends and colleagues, are unchanging and static, and we will not be able to approach personal relationships in an open-minded, positive way.

DEATH

The consideration of death is a very important element in Buddhist mental development. It is one of the cornerstones of Buddhist meditation. The meditation on death is the beginning of serious mental development. The meditation on death really separates the men from the boys in terms of mental development. It is said that from the moment we enter our mother's womb we move towards death. From that moment onwards, every step takes us closer to death. We are like prisoners under sentence of death waiting for the order to come. We are like fish in a net. In one text, it is asked whether we have seen animals at the slaughter house. When the butcher comes to catch a chicken to kill, the others flutter about for a while and rush off to the far side of the pen. When one of them is caught and killed, the others then go back to scratching the ground, looking for kernels of grain. We are all like this. We move inexorably towards death, and yet when we see death, we may be moved perhaps for that moment and then we go about our business. We try our best to forget about death. This is particularly true in the West. In India, there is no attempt made to conceal death. In the West, as soon as someone dies, his corpse is taken off to the mortuary and is dressed up to look better than when he was alive. We all need to recognize the certainty of death. When you meditate on the inevitability of death, think whether there is anyone who has ever escaped death. There is not. There is absolutely no possibility that we will escape death. It is absolutely certain.

While death is absolutely certain, what is absolutely uncertain is when we will die. None of us know when we will die. It is said that life is like a flame in the wind, or like a bubble. It can disappear at any time. Understanding that it is absolutely certain that we will die, but that there is no indication as to when we will die, we should practice self-development without any delay. It is said that if our hair were to catch fire, we would put it out without delay. In the same way, we ought to practice self-development without putting it off because at any time, these opportune conditions may slip away. And if you recall the difficulty of obtaining the human form—the fact that the causes of obtaining the human form are relatively rare, that the number of human beings are relatively few and the nature of human birth - it is important to use this opportunity now. We ought not only to practice the Dharma, but we ought to practice it without delay so that when death comes we will have no cause for regret.

We talked earlier about the three steps of practice— the preparatory practice, the actual practice and the dedicatory practice. The preparatory practice previously discussed was of creating an environment conducive to mental development, because the actual practice was the taking of refuge. The preparatory practice to be discussed at this juncture is the taking of refuge, as it goes for all of the various meditations that we will be considering. From now on, the preparatory practice will be the taking of refuge. This does not mean that you should sit down and meditate in a messy room. It means that the previous instructions are taken for granted. We take refuge to give us stability, institutional support. Meditation on death can be a little bit frightening, so it is helpful to have some support. The refuge formula should be repeated at least three times. Why three? Three is the smallest number of repetitions that one can do that is representative of one's determination, and is representative of many, of being numerous. If you do a thing once maybe you are not serious about it. If you do it twice, it is better, but even numbers are not dynamic, not creative: they are stable and static. Three shows that you really mean it and it is an odd number. It leans towards plurality. The number three may also have been chosen as in ancient Indian languages, we have three numbers—a singular, a dual and a plural, and plural refers to three. Two is not really plural.

MEDITATION ON OPPORTUNE CONDITIONS

Having taken refuge, we go on to consider first the opportune conditions. We should remember as much as we can of these instructions. We consider the rarity of our human situation, and the particular opportunity that we ourselves have. In addition to the eight freedoms and the ten endowments, we have additional advantages. For example, we live in societies which are sufficiently affluent so that we have time to practice the Dharma, we are not required to spend all our time and energy simply to stay alive.

We run this back and forth in our mind. In this respect, in Buddhism, there are three steps to acquiring wisdom. They are study (reading and listening), consideration and meditation. The initial stage is accomplished here—familiarization with the teachings, the methods and the components of the path to self-development. The second step is running this back and forth in one's mind until one gets used to it, until one begins to make it a part of one's mental furniture, one's attitudes. This should not be done in a haphazard way, but rather, after having recited the refuge, we sit and we consider the rarity of the human birth, and particularly the rarity of our own situation. The consideration of the rarity of our own situation is important because in meditation in general, it is no good if it stays out there somewhere. We must link it to our own situation.

MEDITATION ON DEATH

This is also true of the meditation on death. It is not good enough to merely meditate on death in a general abstract way. We must meditate on our own death, on the fact that we will die. Just as we consider the rarity and opportune nature of the human form, here we consider the certainty of death, the fact that no one escapes death, and the uncertainty of the time of death. Having meditated in this way for as long as we are comfortable we then proceed to the concluding phase of the meditation, the dedicatory phase. In this phase, we focus the energy awakened through the meditative practice towards the enlightenment of ourselves and all living beings. A point to note here is that it is important at the beginning not to spend too much time meditating. It is of paramount importance that one be comfortable with the meditation, be happy with the meditation. One should not develop a negative attitude towards the meditation, thinking, "Oh, dear, it is time for me to meditate again. What a nuisance, I can't wait to get it over with." In order that this should not happen, it is better not to spend too much time at first. Ten to fifteen minutes is enough.

There is tension between our contemporary attitudes and the traditional attitudes in regard to the cultivation of these practices of mental development. In the 20th Century, we have come to be very used to the idea of instantaneous results. We want things to happen very quickly. We have instant coffee, TV dinners, etc. There is thus a tendency to want to get through these things quickly. There is a Tibetan teacher in the United States who says that many of us want something very elaborate when we look for meditative techniques. We want helicopters and jet planes. We do not want to walk. This is especially true of many people who come to the Tibetan tradition because of the exotic forms of Tantric meditation. However, even the meditations on death, suffering, impermanence and refuge take up weeks, months and sometimes even years of practice before one takes up the more particular kinds of practices. We are talking here about transforming a way of life, a way of thought. If you have developed certain habits and modes of thinking for twenty or thirty years, these habits cannot be changed in the course of six months or one year. Mental development is effective but it takes time. It is important to begin at the beginning, with the basics. Once these foundations are firmly laid, then more rapid progress can be made.

In order to meditate on the opportune conditions and death, we use the same framework and structure that were described earlier in terms of situation and posture. We use the refuge as a preliminary. We use what we have learned about the opportune conditions, the rarity and precious character of the human form, the certainty of death and the uncertainty of the time of death as the objects of meditation. This takes care of our sitting meditation, our structured or formalized meditation. But as I have been trying to point out, mental development does not stop there. It ought not to be compartmentalized, isolated within that brief space of structured meditation. Meditation should spill over and flood into one's daily life so that eventually it occupies every moment of one's existence. Seeing human beings who are ill or poor, although they have the freedoms and positive endowments can remind one of one's opportunities. In regard to the meditation on death, one can use many opportunities in one's daily life to reflect on the certainty of death and the uncertainty of the time of death, as when one encounters items in the news about individuals in less fortunate conditions or when one sees insects being killed. Also, while sitting among friends one can think that although things are like this now, there will be a time when I will be separated from these people, a time when I will die. When wearing fine clothes, one can think that although I am dressing myself up in fine clothes, there will come a time when this body will decompose. In this way, one maintains a constant awareness of death. This may seem morbid, but it is not. It is a way of achieving a kind of maturity in ones attitude towards one's self, towards one's situation and towards other sentient beings. When we talk about recognition of the facts of life—as, for example, impermanence, certainty of death, etc.—we need to strive for maturity and stability. The meditation on death provides this psychological maturity and stability—as, for instance, people who have a quarrel with someone, perhaps over a very insignificant thing, and then harbor enmity for years and years. A lot of this nurturing of negative energy would be eliminated if people had a mature notion of impermanence and death. It puts a more mature perspective on one's position, and on one's personal relationships. Getting a fancy house seems less important if we realize that we are going to die. Thus, these meditations lead to a psychological maturity, and that is why they are stressed.

III. FRUSTRATION AND KARMA

THE IMPURE EXPERIENCE

The experience of duhkha has often been called the cornerstone or foundation of the teachings of the Buddha. It is the most basic element in the teachings of the Buddha. The reason I cited the original term 'duhkha' is that it is particularly difficult to hit upon a simple translation or term in English that exactly covers the meaning of duhkha. That is why there is a variety of translations used for this term. Some use suffering, others use sorrow, frustration, misery or pain. It really does not matter a great deal, which is used so long as one remains aware of the fact that the term really does have this varied dimension - a whole range of what we would call experiences of tension, unhappiness, and sadness.

We find that this experience of suffering is something which implies not only the superficial and relatively limited sphere of an emotional response, but that it also extends into psychological and meditative areas. So the suffering of mind and body is not only simply that. It is also dissatisfaction, uneasiness and restlessness of mind and body—an unsettled quality about the nature of our experience. We have here three general areas to which the term and concept of duhkha applies. There is the experience of unhappiness, of frustration and pain both mental and physical and of dissatisfaction, unrest or uneasiness.

We can identify the beginning of the role played by

this idea of suffering and frustration in the teachings of the Buddha in the accounts of his early life. Some of the least mythical accounts appear in the Pali Canon. In these accounts, the Buddha reflected upon his experiences before he abandoned the household life. He also reflected upon the struggle for enlightenment. In one of these suttas called the 'Sutta of the Great Effort,' the Buddha talks about the experiences which he had as a youth in his encounter with old age, sickness and death.

There are romanticized accounts of these encounters in the more fanciful biographies of the Buddha. The story is told that the father of the Buddha wished that his son would inherit his kingdom. To guard against the possibility that his son would renounce the world, he took elaborate precautions to protect the young prince from the realities of life, to protect him from the sights of old age, sickness and death. These accounts speak of how the prince matured to early manhood without having encountered these realities of life and how he encountered these sights of old age, sickness and death on his forays out of the palace. But in his own words, the Buddha simply says that, "While I was still a young man, I came upon the figures of old age, sickness and death - an old man, a sick man and a corpse and I felt uneasy. I felt disturbed by this encounter. I thought to myself that this is certainly peculiar in that although I myself am not beyond this situation, that I myself am certainly subject to old age, sickness and death, yet when encountering this situation I felt uneasy, unhappy, I felt disturbed." Having had these experiences, the young prince determined not simply to seek to ignore this problem through the opiate of indulgence in sensual pleasures but rather try to seek a solution to the situation of suffering.

In the biography of the Buddha, we find this early encounter with old age, sickness and death; this suffering which befalls all of us. We all experience this situation in our own life. Certainly we can remember a time in our own life when we first became aware of the reality of death - through the death of a relative or a pet, or became aware of serious incapacitating illness while visiting a relative in the hospital, or having experienced the degradation of old age, etc. So the experience or fact of suffering which is the cornerstone of the Buddha's teachings is an experience which we can all observe or experience for ourselves. It is in a sense the most common experience for all sentient beings, for all conscious life. Descartes in the West began his philosophy with the principle, "I think, therefore I am." But not all living beings are thinking beings. What all living beings have in common is the experience of suffering.

It is in this context that the question is raised in regard to the attitude of Buddhism as a whole—whether it is an optimistic, a pessimistic or a realistic teaching. It is not a sign of optimism to ignore the reality of the situation. The ostrich which buries its head in the sand is not being optimistic. It is simply being foolish. Had the Buddha ended his teachings with suffering, then we could say with justification that the teaching of the Buddha is pessimistic. But although suffering is the starting point of his teachings, the end of suffering is the goal of the Buddha's teachings. If we consider the totality of the Buddha's teachings, we cannot fairly label it pessimistic. In short, the recognition of the reality of suffering, of anxiety, frustration or pain, is an expression of the objective observation of the situation. The use of suffering or frustration as a starting point of a religious, philosophical system used to be a stumbling block in the teaching of Buddhism in the West. It is only when our culture becomes more mature, as we grow out of the rather naive optimism that characterized the first decades of the technological and industrial revolution, that it is easier to come to terms with the realities of the human conditions, to recognize that all is not what we would like it to be.

THE SIX REALMS OF EXISTENCE

Suffering is not confined only to the human situation. It extends to the situation in which all conscious beings find themselves. Here we have the Buddhist conception of samsara, the repeated experience of birth and death in various states of existence.

There are different ways of dividing the cycle of samsara. One popular system used in the Theravada tradition is the division of samsara into thirty-one planes of existence. In the Mahayana, though this division into thirty-one planes is not altogether missing, there is a more common division of this existence into six realms. They are the realm of hell beings, the realm of hungry ghosts, the realm of animals, the realm of human beings, the realm of demi-gods and the realm of gods. All these six realms are characterized by suffering to one degree or another. That is why it is said that the essential characteristic of samsara is suffering, in the same way that the essential characteristic of fire is heat. Here we have to distinguish between essential characteristic and fortuitous characteristic. For example, it is not the essential characteristic of the coffee in the flask to be hot but if it is exposed to the heat of the fire it becomes hot. So the heat of the coffee is acquired, it is not an essential characteristic. But the heat of fire is an intrinsic characteristic of fire. Similarly, suffering is the essential intrinsic characteristic of samsara. This is not only the case in the realm of the hell beings, hungry ghosts, animals and human beings but also in the realms of the demi-gods and gods. The whole of the cycle of sentient existence is characterized by suffering.

This is however not to say that there is no happiness. Certainly there is happiness but that happiness is of a short duration. It will also in a sense become an indirect occasion for suffering through its impermanence. Even that happiness that we experience briefly can become a source of frustration and suffering if we attempt to hold on to it. The reason why we spend so much time contemplating and trying to understand the experience of suffering is to get rid of attachment. The contemplation of suffering is a corrective for the emotional imbalance caused by greed or attachment.

THE THREE CATEGORIES OF SUFFERING

Let us now look at three general divisions of suffering under which we can consider the suffering of the six realms. They are the suffering of suffering, the suffering of change and the suffering of conditioned existence.

The suffering of suffering refers to the experience of suffering found in the three lower realms of existence; that of the hell beings, the hungry ghosts and animals. Suffering of suffering may sound redundant but it conveys rather graphically the image of the redoubling of pain. Suppose you are suffering from a severe headache and someone comes along and knocks you on the head, that is the suffering of suffering, compounded sufferings. The suffering of change refers to the experience of suffering as it is found in the higher realms of human beings, demi-gods and gods. The suffering of conditioned existence refers to the experience of suffering in all the six realms.

1 *Suffering of Suffering*

The realm of the hells incorporates the hot hells, the cold hells and the neighboring hells. In these various hells, the suffering of sentient beings are extremely diverse and intense. The suffering in the hells do not differ in nature from that found in other religions. In the hot hells, we find beings boiled in cauldrons or being cut to pieces by axes and saws. Yet others are imprisoned in burning houses similar in intensity to that of ovens and so forth. In the same way, beings in the cold hells go through extremes of cold unlike anything normally encountered.

The cause of all these sufferings experienced in the hells is ill will or anger. In other words, the result of the negative destructive emotions of ill will, aversion, anger and hatred is rebirth in hells. This is an example of the principle of consonants between cause and effect—hatred, ill-will, anger, cruelty and killing result in rebirth in the hells where one is subjected to hatred, ill-will, anger, cruelty and killing.

The second of the six realms in samsara that participates in this suffering of suffering is the realm of the hungry ghosts. The hungry ghosts are beings who suffer from hunger and thirst, from heat and cold. It is said that certain categories of the hungry ghosts have stomachs the size of a mountain, mouth the size of the eye of the needle, and throat as thin as a hair. So although they are tormented by hunger and thirst, they have great difficulty ingesting any food or liquid. Once they do manage to swallow something, it is as if they have eaten or drunk nothing because the size of the stomach is so vast. Again it is said that these hungry ghosts search here and there for food and water. Sometimes at a great distance they see what they think is a river of fresh water or a mountain of rice. But when they reach the place they find it is only a ribbon of slate and a pile of pebbles. So the suffering of the hungry ghosts is primarily characterized by hunger and thirst.

As in the case of the hell beings, the causes of rebirth as a hungry ghost are similar to the effects. The effects are hunger and thirst and the destitution of desired objects. The causes are greed and avarice. Those who are unable to share, who have no thought except for the continuation of the accumulation of wealth are liable to experience the suffering of the hungry ghosts. Obsessive attachment to possession, wealth and an inability to share result in the deprivation of desired objects.

The third in this category of suffering is the realm of animals. Animals suffer from the killing and eating of one another. Animals are also subject to the depredation of man who kill them for food, for fun, for their skin, teeth and bones. They also suffer from hunger, thirst, heat and cold. There are also various severe sufferings in the realm of animals. Of course, today we have certain animals enjoying a degree of luxury but these cases are relatively rare. They are the result of a certain wholesome energy created in previous lives.

Like the causes of rebirth in the hells and among the hungry ghosts, the causes of rebirth among the animals are similar to the effects. The causes are ignorance and passion. The quality of life, which is wholly obsessed with animal-like pursuits or pleasures, which is devoid of any consideration of development of a more compassionate humanistic vision, creates the conditions for experiencing in the suffering of animals. To put it simply, those who live like animals are liable to experience the suffering of animals.

2 *Suffering of Change*

Even in the more fortunate realms of existence suffering is experienced. In the realm of human beings, human beings experience the suffering of change. There are four major inescapable sufferings - sufferings of birth, old age, sickness and death. Here birth is counted as suffering not only because of the pain we experience in the process of issuing from the womb, but birth is also the gateway to the other sufferings of old age, sickness and death. Once born, the succession of old age, sickness and death is inevitable. Just as the sprout will follow the seed, so birth, old age, sickness and death are the effects of birth in the human realm. In addition to this suffering, we also have other sufferings. The experience of being separated from those whom we love, through the death of a loved one or a temporary separation through an alteration in the person's attitude on a temporary separation through an unavoidable absence, is suffering. We also suffer from coming into contact with those whom we do not get along with. So when we work with a colleague with whom we do not get along, this is suffering. We also suffer from the frustration of desire, from failing to get those things we want, be they material possessions, recognition, prestige, promotion, etc. In short, separation from loved ones, contact with those with whom we cannot get along, and failure to get what we want is suffering.

Not only do human beings suffer but even the demi-gods and gods suffer. Demi-gods are super human beings who enjoy greater power and often greater intelligence than human beings but who do not enjoy the tranquil pleasures of the gods. The demi-gods suffer from jealousy and conflict. Because their situation is inferior to that of the gods, they are jealous of the situation of the gods. They are drawn by their jealousy into conflicts and they suffer as a consequence.

The causes of suffering in the higher realms, just as the causes of suffering in the lower realms, are the negative unwholesome attitudes and actions—greed, ill-will and ignorance. The difference is that in the higher realms, these unwholesome actions are mitigated by wholesome, supportive actions. This too is true in the case of the human realm where the sufferings of human beings are the result of unwholesome actions but they are not so great as the suffering of the beings in the lower realms because they are mitigated by good, wholesome conduct. The demi-gods enjoy a relatively higher position within the cycle of samsara because of wholesome action of generosity performed in the past. But they suffer from jealousy and conflict because of unwholesome actions of envy and quarrels performed in the past.

The gods even though they dwell at the apex of sentient existence, also experience suffering. Why is that so? This is because when the time comes for their departure from the heavens, they suffer unspeakable, incalculable mental anguish. The gods suffer incalculably when they perceive they are about to fall from their lofty perch, when they recognize that the effects of their wholesome positive energy created by them in the past are about to be exhausted and when they perceive that they will be reborn in the human realm or even in the unfortunate realms. The suffering at that point is intensified when they recognize that they have created relatively little if any wholesome karma during their tenure among the gods.

3 Suffering of Conditioned Existence

Thus, all six realms are subjected to suffering—the suffering of suffering, and the suffering of change which contributes to what we call the suffering of conditioned existence. Suffering is characterized by the recognition of the endless activity of birth and death: the endless circling in samsara in which we have been involved since beginning time.

It is said that if all the skeletons of our previous lives were piled up one on top of the other, the heap would be higher than Mount Sumeru, the highest mountain in Buddhist cosmology. If all the mother's milk that we have drunk throughout our countless life times were collected together it would be greater than all the water in all the oceans. The point is that we have been born again and again, endlessly striving to achieve success in our career, to earn our daily bread and so forth, and yet we make no real progress.

There are two important and powerful symbols used in Buddhism—the image of a circle and the image of a spiral. So long as we direct our energies toward conditioned achievements—earning more money, more prestige, even higher rebirth as a god or demi-god, we are perpetuating our existence in this circle. It is only when we produce real renunciation that we begin to break that circle and begin to embark on the spiral which will eventually bring us to something different.

The recognition of the suffering of conditioned existence which in the end has not brought about a qualitative change in the nature of our experience leads to real renunciation. At this stage the wise man should give up all attachments to the cycle of birth and death, in the same way that one would spit spittle out of one's mouth. So the purpose of meditating on suffering is to bring about the correction of the habit of greed, the habit of attachment, the habit of striving in the same old way, all within the circle of samsara.

CAUSES OF SUFFERING

What are the causes of suffering in the six realms? The causes are the afflictions (klesa) and actions (karma). The afflictions are the negative emotional forces—greed, anger and ignorance. The main negative attitude is ignorance. Essentially ignorance is the dichotomy between self and others. Ignorance is the belief in an independent separate existence of subject and object, of I and it, of I and you. We all operate on the assumption of the separate and independent existence of self and others. Once we have this dichotomy between subject and object, we have the basis for the acquisitive and destructive emotional tendencies—the energy of greed and the energy of ill will. So those things which contribute to are beneficial, are pleasurable to the self are sought after, and those things which do not contribute to are not beneficial to the self are rejected. Thus, greed arises with regard to those things which support and sustain the self, and ill will arises with regard to those things which threaten the self.

So here we have the emotional triad with its root, which is ignorance, as the balance point of an inverted triangle. And growing out of that on the one side desire, greed, clinging, attachments (the whole spectrum of acquisitive emotions), and on the other side, ill will, anger, hatred, cruelty, aversion (the whole spectrum of destructive emotions). These lead to actions which are calculated to bring about conditions which are seen to be beneficial to the self, and reject those which are seen to be harmful to self. So these emotions lead to volitional, intentional actions (karma) which in turn leads to the particular characteristic of our existence.

Thus, in general we have two perceptions which together lead to our particular situation in samsara - the illusory perception and the karmic perception. We have the illusory perception which is the perception of subject and object, the separation of self and other. This perception is something which every living being, every conscious being in any of the six realms is caught up in, including the tiniest ant, the most developed of worldly human beings and the highest of the gods. It is common to all sentient existence. In addition to this, we have the karmic perception, that is the result of action. Motivated by greed, anger and delusion, a particular being acts in a particular way, and these actions result in a particular situation in samsara. The karmic energy of our actions stays with us beyond the grave and is carried over to the next life. It clings to us like our shadow. At the point of death, we leave behind loved ones, possessions, every thing but our karma.

Recently, there has been a tendency to interpret the six realms of existence psychologically. In other words, the suffering of hells is in fact the suffering of cruelty, violence, killing and torture as experienced by human beings. The suffering of the hungry ghosts is the suffering of extreme poverty. The situation of the demi-gods is the situation of power and strife experienced by extremely powerful men. The experience of the gods is the experience of tranquil happiness that is felt by human beings. Although this psychological interpretation of these six realms may be a key to understanding the suffering in the six realms, it is not the teachings of the Buddha. In the context of the teaching of the Buddha, the six realms are meant to be accepted to be as real as the human realm. In other words, the experience of the hell-beings, hungry ghosts, animals, etc. are as real as the experience of the human beings. Not withstanding the fact that all these experiences are produced by the mind, they are all equal in reality.

REBIRTH

Rebirth is an idea which many people find difficulty in accepting. The case for rebirth is presented along three general lines. First of all, the Buddha and his foremost disciples testified to having had the ability to recollect their former lives. Their testimony is established in Buddhism. Secondly, we can bring a number of empirical ideas to bear on the question. In attempting to explain peculiar talents and the tendencies of individuals, we find that we have to resort to either some kind of idea of chance or some kind of pre-existence. After all, it is not possible to explain all the diversity among human beings in terms of social conditioning or environment and so forth. So it becomes rather difficult to explain why certain people are constituted in certain ways and the idea of pre-existence, the idea of rebirth supplies this explanation very neatly. Thirdly, increasingly in recent years, there has been a body of evidence acquired by para-psychologists working with hypnotists and spontaneous recollections of previous lives which seems to indicate that rebirth is not an impossibility. Even if we are not prepared now to accept completely the reality of rebirth we can certainly acknowledge that rebirth is a real possibility. Moreover, in the context of this tradition of mental development, belief in rebirth as a working hypothesis contributes to the progress and success of the program of mental development. If we think of this idea of rebirth in these terms, we can begin to approach it without any undue dogmatism.

KARMA

The Buddha taught the efficacy and potency of karma (intentional action) as opposed to the efficacy and potency of any external power, any personal or impersonal force outside man which directs man's destiny. Just as we have the law of action and reaction operating in the physical universe, in the sphere of psychological reality or psychological experience we have the law of karma. Karma in this context is conscious, volitional, intentional action. It is therefore important to note that karma is not simply mechanical action. Rather it is action with intention.

The importance of the mental component of the action cannot be underestimated. The Buddha said that the mind precedes all mental states. All mental states are made of mind. If one speaks or acts with a pure mind, then happiness will follow. If one acts or speaks with an impure mind, then suffering will follow. So the six realms in samsara are the result of the mind, the result of mental energy or intention. All of our experiences are the result of intention, which in its final stage finds its expression in actions. For example, when we decide to reach out our arm to hold a cup. It is only in the last stage of our volitional mental process that the arm actually extends itself and takes hold of the cup. This is the materialization of the intention that goes before it. Karma is this kind of intentional action. Actions that are performed unintentionally do not constitute potent karma.

Through volitional intentional actions, we shape our destiny. Thus, our body and our situation in the world is the result of the materialization of the karmic energy. The intentional action which we performed in the past has conditioned our present situation, and the intentional actions performed now together with those of the past condition our future. This is how karma operates—with an element from the past and an element that is constantly being supplied by the present. There is thus a kind of matrix, a kind of intersection of conditionality and freedom. The situation that we find ourselves in at this moment is the result of past actions, but we are always free at this moment to change that direction as a result of new intentional actions.

FOUR KINDS OF KARMA

There are four kinds of karma. They are reproductive karma, supportive karma, counteractive karma and destructive karma. These four kinds of karma together shape and determine the course of a given life. The reproductive karma gives the general nature of the present life. The supportive karma enhances or supports that general tone, the general character of our present life. Counteractive karma weakens, disturbs or hinders the general direction of that life, while destructive karma destroys or interrupts that direction.

Traditionally, the case of the Buddha's cousin Devadatta is used to illustrate the functioning of these four kinds of karma. We have Devadatta's reproductive karma, which is generally of a wholesome or fortunate nature. He was born with many endowments. He was born as a human being, and was also born into a noble family. The karma that he had generated in his previous life is generally wholesome, and that reproductive karma sets the stage for the present life. His supportive karma enhances that general tone. As a young man, he joined the Order to become a monk. This is a further wholesome karma which supports the general character of his reproductive karma. But then in his later life, Devadatta instigated a schism in the Order of monks because of jealousy and selfishness. This is counteractive karma as this karma modified the generally wholesome reproductive and supportive karma. Finally, when Devadatta attempted to kill the Buddha, we have a manifestation of destructive karma, karma which brings about the end of his favorable situation. Thus, there are four kinds of karma—two kinds giving the general character of life and two kinds opposing that general tone.

But it does not necessarily mean that the first two kinds have to be good and the second two kinds have to be bad. For example, if one's reproductive karma is bad one is born in extreme poverty, not having access to education and so forth. The supportive karma of that reproductive karma would support the generally negative character of the reproductive karma, like indulging in sexual misconduct or dealing in slaves in one's early life. The counteractive and destructive karma would be the karma which runs counter to the general character of the reproductive and supportive karma. Thus, we have these four kinds of karma which sets the stage, enhances, counteracts and eventually destroys the general direction, and to a greater or lesser extent they operate in an individual's life. In some cases, there may be relatively little counteractive karma. In others, the destructive karma may be absent. There will nonetheless always be the reproductive karma which gives the general character to this present life.

SHORT-TERM AND LONG-TERM KARMA

The effects of karma may be experienced in this life, in the next life, or after many, many lives. So in saying that the law of karma is a counterpart to the law of action and reaction that operates in this physical universe, we mean that we can see a parallel with the law of action and reaction that operates in physics. In this respect, we can see a certain parallel with the law of conservation of energy, in that the effects of karma need not necessarily be immediate. Their occurrence depends on the combination of causes and conditions. They may occur immediately or they may occur only after an intervening period. We can see this parallelism too in very prosaic examples. For instance, if we plant seeds of watermelons and cucumbers, we can have the fruits in the space of a few months. But in the case of other plants like walnuts and durians we will have the fruits only after many years. In the same way — karma has short-term and long-term results.

WEIGHT OF KARMA

The law of karma is a very carefully balanced system. It is not a simple-minded doctrine. An intentional action can be divided into several stages—the initial intention, the action, and the completion of the action. Intention by itself carries a certain weight. Intention combined with action carries a greater weight. Intention, action and completion together carry the greatest weight. So, for example, one may intend to kill but one may not act upon that intention.

This will carry a certain karmic weight. But if one has the intention to kill and one actually acts upon the intention, the weight of that karma will be greater. And if the action is completed in that it results in the death of the victim, then that karma will carry the fullest weight.

There are even more refined systems for gauging the strength of karma. One of these systems uses five factors to gauge the weight of karma. The five factors are divided into two categories—the subjective category and the objective category. In other words, the factors that have to do with the doer (or the agent) of the action, and the factors that have to do with the object or the being towards whom the action is directed.

The first of the factors is persistence or repeated actions. Thus, an isolated action does not have the weight that a repeated one has. If one performs a particular action once in a while, it has less weight than if one performs it all the time. The second factor is intention. If one performs a particular action with a great intention, it has more weight than if one performs it without intention or little intention. Thirdly, if one performs an action without reluctance or regret, this will have greater weight. These are the three factors in the category which has to do with the condition of the agent of the action. A concrete example of this is that of a person who persistently kills, who persistently kills with a great resolve to kill, and whose killing is unopposed by reluctance or regret.

There are two factors regarding the object towards whom the action is directed. The first is the quality or status of the object and the second is the nature of the relationship between the object and the doer of the action.

For example, if one kills a Buddha, the force of that action is much greater than if one were to kill an ant. And if one kills one's parent or some one who has benefited one, then the weight of the action is greater than if one kills a mosquito which has given one malaria. Thus, it is not only the subjective situation, the situation of the doer of the action which determines the weight of the karma, but also the objective situation, the status of the beings and their relationship. It is in this way that the actual weight of karma is weighed, taking into consideration the subjective and objective factors. It is also in this way that the general weight of karma determines and shapes one's situation. So one need not be afraid if one accidentally kills an ant.

UNWHOLESOME ACTIONS

In order to understand karma we need to look at three areas. We need to look at the nature of karma; the effects of karma and the application of what we have learnt by looking at the nature and effects of karma.

With regard to the nature of karma, karma is of three general kinds—unwholesome, wholesome and neutral. Unwholesome karma is intentional action that is motivated by the three negative, emotional energies of ignorance, greed and anger. It is said that just as a poisonous seed will give rise to a poisonous plant, so unwholesome actions done with these three kinds of motivation will give rise to suffering or unhappiness.

In all, there are ten unwholesome actions—three of body, four of voice and three of mind. The three of body, are killing, stealing and sexual misconduct. Sexual misconduct entails the violation of the principle of respect for personal relationship and respect for the person. If a certain defined and accepted relationship exists between two individuals, as for instance the relationship of marriage, then a sexual act which betokens a lack of regard for that relationship is categorized as sexual misconduct. An example of the violation of the principle of respect for a person is forcible sexual misconduct that transgresses respect for a person's integrity. So sexual intercourse, as defined in Buddhism does not preclude in a formalistic way any specific kind of relationship. But it does encourage respect for personal relationship and respect for personal integrity.

The four unwholesome actions of voice are lying; slandering or backbiting; harsh and abusive speech; and idle, malicious talk. Idle talk does not mean that we cannot even talk about the weather. It implies amusing ourselves with the weaknesses, shortcomings and misfortunes of others. In short, amusing ourselves at the expense of others.

The three unwholesome actions of the mind are greed, anger and deluded views. It means wanting the good things that others are enjoying, wishing misfortune on others and having deluded misguided views.

The fruits or effects of these unwholesome actions are of four kinds. Firstly, we have the fully matured fruit, the complete effect of which is rebirth in the appropriate three lower realms. The fully matured fruit of the action motivated by anger is rebirth in the hells, action motivated by greed results in rebirth as a hungry ghost, and the action motivated by ignorance results in rebirth among the animals. Secondly, the effect can be experienced in a manner similar to the action without necessarily having the complete effect of rebirth in the unhappy realm. For example, if the act of killing does not have its full weight it will result in a shorter life, in fear and in separation from loved ones if a person is born as a human being. These are effects which are similar to the cause—killing which is depriving others of life resulting in shorter life, fear, paranoia, etc. Another example of the effect being similar to the cause is the case of stealing. Even if the person is not reborn as a hungry ghost, stealing will result in poverty, in an inability to earn one's independent livelihood. The third form in which the effect of the action can be experienced is the reinforcement of habit. Killing performed in a former life will result in a tendency to kill in this life. Finally, the effect can be felt in the condition of one's environment. So although one may be born as a human being and not in a lower realm, one's circumstances will be prejudiced by past unwholesome actions. So, for example, if one has practiced a lot of killing, one may be born in an environment where the climate is conducive to fear.

It is in these four ways that the effects of karma are experienced. All the unhappiness and suffering that we experience is the result of unwholesome actions. Knowing this, one ought to strive to abandon unwholesome actions. By doing this, one can alter the balance of one's karma. One can change the nature of one's experience from an unhappy situation to a happier situation. This may take some time but there is no doubt that it will eventually happen.

WHOLESOME ACTIONS

Just as unwholesome actions are those actions activated by the three negative emotions, wholesome actions are actions which are done in the absence of those negative emotions. Wholesome actions are like medicinal seeds that result in medicinal fruits. They will bring about happiness.

Wholesome actions are those actions motivated by the opposite of the three afflictions. Rather than actions motivated by greed, we have actions which are motivated by renunciation or detachment. Rather than actions motivated by ill will, we have actions motivated by love and compassion. Rather than actions motivated by ignorance, we have actions motivated by wisdom.

These positive motivations will lead to the performance of wholesome actions like generosity, compassion and so forth. These wholesome actions will bear either the full-fledge results—that is, rebirth among men, demi-gods, or gods, or results that are similar to the causes as, for example, protection of life yields long life, acts of generosity yield wealth. Reinforcement of positive habits like generosity will reinforce and create the foundation for repealed acts of generosity in the subsequent life and so forth. Finally, one's environment will be conducive as a result of virtuous, wholesome actions done in the past.

Just as understanding unwholesome actions and their effects ought to lead us to renounce unwholesome actions, so understanding wholesome actions and their effects ought to lead us to cultivate wholesome actions. It is in this context that it is said that we ought not to spurn small wholesome action as there is a tendency sometimes to think that it is such a tiny good deed that it may not be worth doing. We may prefer to do very dramatic and conspicuous good deeds but even droplets of water will eventually fill a bucket.

NEUTRAL ACTIONS

Neutral actions are actions either done without intention

such as the accidental stepping on an insect, or actions done which have no particular moral consequences. That is, they do not impinge on the existence and happiness of other beings. Actions of this category include walking, sleeping, travelling and handicraft work. These are called neutral or ineffective actions because they produce no karma. Special attention is paid to neutral actions because we spend a lot of our time involved in neutral actions. Why should all this time go to waste? Why do we not transform these neutral actions into intentional wholesome actions through the power of our mind? After all, karma is intentional action, and the mental component is very important in karma.

There are specific techniques used to transform these neutral actions into wholesome actions through the conscious awakening of the intention as in the case of dedication of merits wherein through a conscious directing of energy one can focus wholesome energy to a particular purpose. So when we leave our home for work, we can turn neutral actions into wholesome actions by thinking "Just as I leave my home now, may all beings tread the path to enlightenment, may all beings commence on that process of self-development." In the same way, just as one returns to one's home after work, one can think "Just as I now return home, may all beings achieve the goal of self-development, may all beings achieve enlightenment." Again, when involved in cleaning, one can think "As I clean these dishes, may all beings purify themselves of the afflictions of greed, anger and delusion." When meeting another person one may think "As I meet this person, may all beings meet an enlightened person." Again as one goes to sleep, one may think "Just as I go to sleep may all beings achieve the Dharmakaya" and when one awakens, one can think "May all beings achieve the Rupakaya." In this way, we can gradually transform neutral actions into wholesome actions. This is called meditation in action. Through these techniques, we can accelerate our progress along the path of mental development.

INTERDEPENDANT ORIGINATION

Karma, together with the negative emotions, lead to the particular situation in which we find ourselves. In very broad terms, this is the Buddhist teaching of interdependent origination. Classically, this is formulated in terms of twelve components. It often happens that one loses sight of the forest for the trees if one embarks upon this kind of treatment of interdependent origination. Broadly, interdependent origination can be divided into three general components—afflictions (klesa), actions (karma) and rebirth and suffering (duhkha). The afflictions of greed, anger and delusion lead to action (karma). The afflictions and karma together lead to rebirth and suffering in the six realms. The experience of suffering in the six realms reinforces these afflictions—the habit of desire, the habit of ill will and the habit of dichotomizing between self and other. Thus, we have a circular pattern wherein the negative emotions condition actions, actions condition rebirth and suffering which in turn reinforces the afflictions. Our existence is not an independent existence, it is an existence conditioned by klesa and karma. As a result of the combination of afflictions and actions we exist in a particular way. This is how rebirth takes place.

What this implies is that our existence is an existence which is characterized by the fact of not-self. There is no identical essence that exists throughout a series of lives. In other words, there is no substantial personality that existed in my former life or will exist in my subsequent life. The river has continuity but it does not have identity, it is neither the same nor different. It is in this sense that interdependent origination is existence dependent upon klesa and karma. It avoids the two alternatives. It avoids the alternative of identity and permanence on one hand, and it avoids the alternative of difference and of discontinuity on the other hand.

Let me use an example to illustrate this. When a teacher instructs a student, the student acquires the material transmitted to him by the teacher. But the knowledge acquired by the student and the knowledge of the teacher are not the same. There is no substantial identity between the knowledge of the teacher and the knowledge of the student. Yet the knowledge of the teacher is the cause of the knowledge now possessed by the student. Again, when an image is reflected by the mirror, the image in the mirror is not identical to the object, and yet the image in the mirror is the effect of the object. So it is neither identical nor altogether different. The image is conditioned by the subject.

The same kind of relationship exists between this life and the next life. This particular life is the cause of the suffering of the subsequent life. It conditions the next life. In this sense, we have the continuity of cause and effect.

MEDITATION ON FRUSTRATION AND KARMA

In order to meditate on suffering and karma, we use the materials already covered. We personalize the materials. When we contemplate on suffering, we think of the suffering in the six realms and we think especially what it would be like if we were to experience it for ourselves. Then we think especially of our own situation, the sufferings we experience in our own situation.

When we contemplate on karma, we think of wholesome and unwholesome actions. We especially recall that it is the unwholesome actions we have committed in the past which have become the cause of our unhappiness and suffering here and now. Recognizing this, we particularly strive to bring about a real renunciation. We resolve to give up unwholesome actions.

IV. LOVE AND COMPASSION

THE EXPERIENCE OF TRANSFORMATION

In our treatment previously of the suffering of the six realms and the law of karma, we have completed the material which is representative of the impure vision—the illusory vision which is the vision motivated by the dichotomy of self and other, and the karmic experience which is the specific form that one's existence takes shaped by one's karma. They are the impure vision because they are concerned with suffering and the causes of suffering— unwholesome actions motivated by the negative mental emotions of greed, anger and delusion. The impure vision is ameliorated by a development of detachment or renunciation and it is for this purpose of the development of detachment that we considered the suffering of the six realms and the causes of suffering.

Just as in the case of the impure vision the task was the cultivation of detachment, in the case of the experience of transformation the primary task is the cultivation of love, compassion, and the enlightenment thought or mind. This cultivation removes the other fundamental negative emotions in that whereas the cultivation of detachment removes greed and desire, the cultivation of love and compassion removes ill-will and anger, and the cultivation of the enlightenment thought and wisdom removes ignorance. Now we begin to move beyond the initial stage of loosening the bond of attachment towards the goal of total transformation of our experience. We shall talk about the first process in the experience of transformation — the cultivation of love and compassion.

Love and compassion directly removes ill-will and anger and they indirectly weaken attachment to the self. This is because in so far as we cultivate the ideal of the sameness of all living beings which are implicit in the cultivation of love and compassion, we begin to weaken the ego, though this will only be directly confronted and removed at the stage of cultivating the enlightenment thought or mind.

The importance of love and compassion has been recognized not only in the tradition we are considering, but also both within and without the whole Buddhist tradition. It is said in the Buddhist tradition that one who cultivates love and compassion will find happiness wherever one goes. In the same way that by covering the feet with leather it is as if the whole surface of the earth is covered with leather, likewise, the mind which is infused with love and compassion will encounter well-being wherever it goes.

As is the case with virtually all the fundamental teachings of Buddhism, we find the early examples for these practices of love and compassion in the life of the Buddha. If we examine the biographical accounts of the Buddha's life, we will come across a large number of incidents which vividly express the Buddha's quality of love and compassion. One of these is the incident concerning a bird and a worm. In the Pali tradition, we find the account of the Buddha's attendance at a ploughing ceremony when he was a child. In the process of ploughing the earth, a worm was turned up.

Upon this happening, a bird swooped down from the sky, caught the worm in its beak and gobbled up the worm. There are other accounts in which this is elaborated. According to the Mahayana tradition, it was a frog which was turned up by the ploughing and it was a snake that devoured the frog. Whatever the version, the point is quite clear. It is a predatory cycle wherein living beings sustain themselves by killing other living beings. The contemplation of this incident led the young prince to ruminate on the suffering of life and to recognize the need to find some way to eliminate this cycle of suffering.

Later, in the career of the Buddha, there is the story of the sick monk Tissa who came down with an infectious disease and whom the other members of the monastic community were loathed to care for because of the infectious nature and the particularly disgusting character of the disease. The Buddha took upon himself to care for the sick member of the Order. With his own hands, he cleaned and dressed the sores.

ESSENCE OF THE MAHAYANA

I have spoken about the transition from the initial movement of detachment to a secondary movement of positive development. This is exemplified in the two general schemes of ethical-moral conduct within the Buddhist tradition. These schemes were indicated by the Buddha himself when he summarized his teachings with regard to action by saying, "Refrain from harming others, do good, try to benefit others. These two great fundamental principles are also reflected in the two great moral codes that we find in Buddhism—the pratimoskha percepts (which have to do with individual liberation and which is essentially a negative code as the precepts are concerned with avoiding harming others), and the

Bodhisattva commitments or vows which are the positive concomitants of the negative code of the Pratimoskha as the vows concern helping others. The essence of these Bodhisattva vows which are prescribed for those whose primary concern is the alleviation of the suffering not only of oneself but of all is the injunction to help others whenever possible.

This is the primary orientation of the Mahayana. And we can see the beginning of the Mahayana again in the career of the Buddha Sakyamuni because we are told that after his enlightenment he spent a number of weeks in the vicinity of Bodhagaya. Two very significant events occurred during this period. First of all, the Buddha was said to have been tempted by Mara (the symbol of sensual desire, death and decay) to enter nirvana straight away. It is significant that it is treated in this tradition as a temptation. What we have here really is the presentation of a choice, biographically for the Buddha, but philosophically a choice for all who are interested in the Buddhist tradition and that is the choice of seeking freedom for oneself or seeking freedom for all living things. The Buddha regarded the seeking of personal freedom as a temptation and he chose not to do that. He decided to teach his experience of enlightenment to those who are able to appreciate it. The willingness to put aside one's own personal freedom for the liberation of all sentient beings can be seen as the beginning of the essential orientation of the Mahayana. This is why it is said that compassion is the essence of the Mahayana.

SAMENESS OF ALL LIVING BEINGS

This idea of love and compassion in the Mahayana and in Buddhism as a whole is founded upon the recognition of the fundamental equality or sameness of all living beings. The simplest way to formulate this idea is by saying that each and every one of us wants to be happy and avoid suffering. This is universally true, whether we speak of the condition of human beings, animals or other forms of conscious existence. Being conscious is synonymous with wanting to have happiness and to avoid suffering. Just as I wish to be happy and to avoid pain, likewise, all other living beings too wish to be happy and wish to avoid pain. Incidentally, this is not only the foundation of cultivation of love and compassion but is also the foundation of Buddhist ethics and morality. This is because the general principle of not harming others enjoins certain general form of conduct —avoid stealing, lying, sexual misconduct. All of these are founded upon this basic recognition of the sameness and equality of self and others. Just as I do not want to be killed, robbed, etc., likewise, all other sentient beings do not want to be killed, robbed, etc. This basic equality has been recognized by other religious teachers as for example Confucius and Jesus.

POSITIVE SOCIAL EMOTIONS

Love and compassion appear in the Buddhist tradition in two related but distinguishable contexts—the Four Immeasurables (Brahmavihara) or what I have called the positive social emotions, and the awakening of the enlightenment thought or mind. The Four Brahmavihara are love, compassion, sympathetic or altruistic joy, and equanimity. They are called social emotions because they refer to social existence. Here we need to understand social existence not only in terms of our human existence, but also in terms of sentient existence that includes all the other forms of existence as well. They are called limitless meditations or attitudes because sentient beings are limitless in number. What we are talking about here is a movement from ordinary limited love and compassion, sympathetic joy and equanimity to great, limitless love and compassion, sympathetic joy and equanimity.

The best way to illustrate these positive emotions is to take a couple of examples from ordinary daily life. We experience love at one time or another—love for our relatives, love for another human being, love for a pet, etc. In the Buddhist context, this kind of love is the wish that the object towards whom our love is directed be well and happy. This kind of love is limited. It is not sublime love because it is limited or circumscribed to a particular individual or group. Although this supplies the basis upon which we can cultivate great love, at this stage it is not limitless love. The same is true of compassion. We have all felt the wish to relieve ourselves and others of suffering. While this is an example of compassion, this is not an example of limitless compassion. Again, this is true of sympathetic joy. When our friends or relatives achieve success. It is because we identify with them and consider them a part of us that we experience sympathetic joy. But so long as it is confined to a certain individual or group, it is not great sympathetic joy. Again with equanimity, we may feel a certain detachment towards those whom we do not know well but it is not great detachment because it is not extended to all sentient beings without exception. The cultivation of the positive social emotions involves the gradual extension of these emotions in their limited form in daily life to include all sentient beings. That extension is possible because of this fundamental sameness of all sentient beings. There are particular techniques for extending these positive social emotions, which I will subsequently cover.

AWAKENING THE BODHICHITTA

Cultivating love and compassion are the first steps in awakening the enlightenment thought or mind (Bodhicitta). What is the Bodhicitta? The Bodhicitta is the aspiration to achieve freedom not for oneself but for the sake of all sentient beings. One who has this aspiration is a Bodhisattva. The benefit of both self and other has always been important in Buddhism. There is the story of three monks who encountered a murderer in the forest. They had three choices. One of them said "Kill me and spare the other two." The second monk said. "I will run away. Kill the other two." The third monk said, "No one should die. Let us sit down and talk it over." The objective of Buddhism has always been not only the benefit of self, nor only the benefit of others, but the benefit of both self and others. Both self and others should benefit. This can be seen in the context of the enlightenment thought as well. If in the context of ordinary daily life, the goal of Buddhism is the achievement of the goal of self and other, how much more true will it be that in regard to the ultimate good, the goal should not be the achievement of the transformed state for self alone but for self and others.

One of the most common reservations regarding the possibility and practicability of this achievement of enlightenment for the sake of all living beings is that it is too difficult a task. The Mahayana's view is that once we awaken this aspiration to free all sentient beings from suffering, our progress in fact becomes easier. Why?

Because by orienting our practice towards all sentient beings, all sentient beings will become our helpers. This is worked out quite specifically in the Mahayana where, it is said that in practicing the perfections of the Bodhisattva path, the practice of generosity is enhanced by sentient beings because they provide us the opportunity to practice giving. This is also true in regard to the practices of good conduct and patience. All sentient beings help and cooperate. Rather than making spiritual development more difficult, the orientation of one's practice towards the universal emancipation of all living beings in fact makes it easier because it involves all sentient beings as participants in this progress towards the goal of enlightenment.

HOW TO DEVELOP LOVE

It is recognized in the Buddhist tradition that to develop universal love and compassion may not be easy. It is therefore suggested that one begin the process where it is easier to do so, where there is an emotional readiness for this attitude of love and compassion. It is suggested that one begin with one's mother irrespective of whether she is alive or dead. I have come across people who have not had a particularly close bond of affection for their mothers. In these cases, one ought to begin with some other person. In most cases, however, there is a very strong feeling of love for one's mother.

One begins one's cultivation of love and compassion with one's mother. In order to do this, one ought to bring one's mother to mind, visualize one's mother before one and think of her great kindness. This is worked out in great detail. One ought to think of one's situation at birth, that one was totally helpless at birth. We were unable to feed and clean ourselves. We would have died had it not been for the care and attention of our mother. Our mother not only cared for us after the time of our birth but even prior to our birth, at the cost of great discomfort to herself. She carried us in her womb for nine months. She underwent a great deal of pain to bear us. She then protected us and nurtured us through the early period of our life, cleaning the dirt from our body with her own hands, feeding us and washing us, always thinking only of our benefit. This pattern continued into later life. It was our mother who taught and helped us to walk, to sit, and to interact with others. It was always her concern that we had sufficient food and clothing, that we be educated. In other words, at all times she was intimately concerned with our welfare and benefit. And it was because of the kindness of our mother that we were able to grow up into mature and independent beings.

I have previously mentioned a number of examples to illustrate the number of repeated lives that we all have. In this context every living being has at one time or another been our mother and in each of these former lives our mother has been kind to us. This is true in whatever realm we happened to have been born. In fact, it is fundamental to Mahayana teachings that all living beings have been our kind mothers.

This is a way of taking the feeling of love, which we have, for our mother in this life and extending it to all sentient beings. This is true of sentient beings whom we do not recognize in this life, of sentient beings who have been our enemies and also of sentient beings who are not humans, the beings in the other realms of existence. So those people whom we see in the buses, or on the streets, although we do not recognize them because of the changes that they have all undergone over the course of countless lifetimes, each and every one of them has benefited us. We have a very close and indissoluble bond of interdependence that binds us to all sentient beings throughout these countless lifetimes.

How can we repay the kindness of our mother in this very life and the kindness of countless sentient beings? The only way to repay them is to see that they have happiness and the causes of happiness. This wish that they have happiness and the causes of happiness is the meaning of the cultivation of love. How are we to do that? Simply by giving them material things will not make them happy and certainly will not supply them with the causes of happiness. In the scriptures, it is said that even if we were to carry our parents on our shoulders day and night for an entire lifetime, this would not be sufficient to repay the kindness of our parents. Even if we were to offer our parents the entire universe with all its riches, this would not be sufficient. The only way we can repay our parents and all sentient beings is to achieve Buddhahood. This is because by achieving Buddhahood we will be able to show them how to achieve happiness and the causes of happiness up to and including the supreme bliss of enlightenment.

In our specific meditation for cultivating great love and compassion, we begin with our mother in this life. We picture her before us. We think of her kindness and we arouse a very strong wish that she be happy and she have the causes of happiness. From our mother, we move on to develop this attitude towards our father, our relatives, and our friends. Then we go on to cultivate this attitude towards strangers for whom we do not have any particular feeling of closeness. Finally, we extend this feeling of love to our enemies, recalling that although in this life they may be our enemies, in fact in a previous life they were kind to us. Perhaps it is because in the previous life we did not reciprocate their kindness so that in this life they have become our enemies.

It is said that the anger and hostile actions of other sentient beings ought to be regarded as the hostile actions of our friends and relatives in this life when they are temporarily demented by disease. If, for example, you have a very close friend who had too much to drink, and who wanted to punch you, you would not allow him to do it. But at the same time, you would not become angry with him because you recognize that this person has been a good friend to you but is now temporarily demented. You would cope with the situation not by becoming angry and heating him up. In the same way, the hostile actions of other sentient beings should be regarded as the temporary effect of the madness caused by the impurities of mind.

One goes on to extend this universal love and compassion to all sentient beings, not only those who inhabit the human realm, but also to those who inhabit the other five realms of existence. If it is difficult to meditate on this kind of love towards the hell-beings, hungry ghosts, and animals, an expedient means is to visualize these beings to be in the form of human beings. Again, if anger should arise when we meditate on love towards our enemies, we can recall the example I have mentioned. We can also recall the faults of anger, that it is the primary cause of rebirth in the hells. By keeping this in mind, we can avoid the obstacles in the way of developing this feeling of universal love towards all sentient beings.

HOW TO DEVELOP COMPASSION

After we have developed universal love, we go on to develop universal compassion towards all sentient beings. Just as love is the wish that all sentient beings be happy and have the causes of happiness, so compassion is the wish that all living beings be free from suffering and from the causes of suffering. Just as the causes of happiness are wholesome actions, the causes of suffering are unwholesome actions.

The techniques for cultivating universal compassion are similar to what I have outlined in the case of the cultivation of universal love. We begin with our kind mother. We extend this feeling of compassion to our mother, this wish that our mother be free from suffering and the causes of suffering. We extend this feeling to strangers, enemies, and all sentient beings based upon our understanding of the fact that all sentient beings have at one time or another been our kind mothers.

THE IMPORTANCE OF COMPASSION

The essence of the Mahayana is compassion. The importance of compassion in the Mahayana can be seen very explicitly in many Mahayana teachings. It is said, for example, that universal compassion is the chief cause of achieving enlightenment. It is the mother of Buddhahood. The state of Buddhahood is born out of compassion. It is said that those who wish to achieve enlightenment need only to cultivate universal compassion. All the perfections of the path of Buddhahood will come along naturally as a matter of course. Just as when one invites a king to one's home for a meal, it goes without saying that he will come with his retinue. In the same way, by cultivating universal compassion, all the other practices of the Bodhisattva path

—generosity, good conduct, patience, energy, meditation and wisdom—will come along. Why? This is because it is universal compassion that impels us to achieve Buddhahood in order to relieve all sentient beings permanently of their suffering. So although we cultivate universal love and universal compassion, we cannot achieve this goal of relieving all sentient beings permanently of suffering without ourselves having achieved Buddhahood. Giving material objects or ordinary skills will not secure happiness and the freedom from suffering. Only the qualities of a Buddha—skilful means and wisdom—can enable us to achieve the highest goal of all living beings, their permanent happiness and their permanent freedom from suffering. That is why it is said that compassion is the beginning, the middle and the end of the progress towards Buddhahood. Compassion is the seed of the awakening of the enlightenment thought. It is the first condition in that it is the practice of the perfections which eventually leads to the fruition of the Bodhisattva practices, in the fruit of Buddhahood. And it is also the end in that compassion is the essence of the fruit of Buddhahood. It is the compassion of the Buddha which motivates his participation in the sphere of phenomena in order to lead all sentient beings to Buddhahood.

THREE-FOLD COMPASSION

In the cultivation of compassion, there are three levels of compassion. In considering this we have already an indication of a further transition, beyond the mere cultivation of universal love and compassion, to the correction of the negative emotion of anger and ill will. We begin to enter the domain of the cultivation of wisdom which corrects the fundamental error of dichotomizing self and other which is the nature of ignorance. We begin to move beyond this because in considering the three-fold compassion, we have a movement from compassion cultivated towards sentient beings to compassion cultivated in the absence of sentient beings.

1 Compassion Towards Beings

The first stage of this three-fold compassion is already familiar to us. It is the wish that all sentient beings be free from suffering and from the causes of suffering. Seeing the suffering of sentient beings, we wish to free them from their suffering. On this level, we have a belief in the real existence of sentient beings as individuals and we have a belief in the reality of their suffering. This is a relatively simple, naively realistic conception.

2 Compassion Towards Elements

This is followed by compassion towards factors of experience. What this means is that in actual fact these sentient beings whom we naively assume to be unitary wholes are in fact not unitary, not independent. They are in fact collections of factors of experience (skandhas). The personality is not unitary, independent. It is conditioned. It is a collection of processes. Here we begin to enter the domain of analytical wisdom. We begin to attack ignorance by an analysis which dissects that personality into its component parts. These parts are the aggregates or factors of experience—the physical factors of experience (physical body, the material objects around us like the trees, tables, etc.) and the mental factors of experience (feeling, perception, recognition, ideas). A collection of these physical and mental factors make up the personality.

Why do people suffer? Here is the connection with compassion. Understanding this composite collective nature of the personality helps us to understand the causes of suffering. The fundamental cause of suffering is self-clinging. It is assuming the reality of a unitary, independent self as opposed to the material objects around it. It is this dichotomy of self and other that sets up this stressful situation wherein we have anger, desire and greed. If there were no separation between self and other, there would be neither anger nor greed. Towards whom or what would we be angry or desirous? If there were no idea of an independent self, there would be no idea of a gulf between self and other. When we begin to understand self analytically as a collection of physical and mental factors of experience, we begin to undermine the cause of suffering, that idea of self which is the cause of suffering.

It is said that taking this collection of physical and mental factors of experience to be the self is like taking a rope on the floor in the darkness to be a snake. Because of the condition of semi-darkness we are liable to mistake the rope to be a snake. Having mistaken the rope for a snake, we will experience fear and discomfiture. In the same way, because of the failure to apply the light of analytical investigation, we take the factors of experience to be an independent personality and for that reason we experience the negative emotions of anger, greed, etc. Compassion with regard to the factors of experience is the second aspect of the three-fold compassion. Here we begin to see that the suffering of sentient beings is due to their ignorance, mistaking the physical and mental processes to be the personality.

3 *Objectless Compassion*

We move on to what is called objectless compassion. Understanding that the personality is a collection of physical and mental factors of experience analytically implies a dissection of the notion of personality. When we go on to understand that these factors are interdependent, that the personality exists in relation to the interaction of all these physical and mental processes, we then arrive at the unreality of the self. So in the final analysis the self does not exist. It does not exist in an absolute way. But it exists relative to causes and conditions. In truth, a personality does not exist absolutely. That means that these sentient beings towards whom we cultivate great love and compassion in actuality do not exist. In other words, we cultivate love and compassion towards sentient beings whom we know through insight not to exist in truth.

If they do not exist in truth, if their suffering is the result of their illusion, why do we cultivate this objectless compassion? The reason is that the suffering of that person who takes the rope for a snake is real to him even though we may know that the snake in the final analysis does not exist. He is genuinely distressed by that experience even though we may know from our vantage point that in fact the snake does not exist. So objectless compassion is cultivated for the benefit of relieving these sentient beings who have not yet kindled the light of analytical wisdom.

This can be illustrated by means of an ordinary example. Suppose you happen to be asleep and you happen to experience a nightmare. Suppose you dream that you were trapped in a burning building from which there is no escape. You will experience a high degree of fear and discomfiture. You will toss and turn about. When you awake, you will be relieved to know that you are safe and sound in your bed, and that the experience which you had in the dream was unreal. Suppose the following night you happen to see your spouse tossing and turning about in bed, muttering "Fire, Fire" obviously in great distress. What will your reaction be? Will you simply lie back smiling to yourself thinking that this fear is totally baseless, or will you reach out to awaken that person because of the recognition that for him or her that discomfiture is real. This is compassion in operation. This is the union of compassion and wisdom. While we know through analytical wisdom that suffering arises because of a fundamental error, yet we know that phenomenalogically suffering is real for those who are trapped in that error. So we cultivate objectless compassion. We also see this in children. They experience great distress over trivial matters as when a penny balloon is burst. We know from our vantage point as adults that that loss is a trivial matter but we still make a spontaneous effort out of compassion to identify with the suffering of the child in order to relieve the suffering.

EXCHANGING SELF AND OTHER

I said earlier that because of the reliance upon the principle of the equality of self and other, the cultivation of love and compassion indirectly attacks the notion of self. At its highest limit, objectless compassion directly impinges upon the area of the cultivation of wisdom and removal of the self/other dichotomy. We already have begun to undermine the idea of self and we see this very clearly illustrated in the practice which Shantideva called the wholly secret of the teachings of the Buddha. He said that those who wish to reach Buddhahood quickly ought to cultivate this practice.

This practice is called the exchange of self and other. What this means is that having cultivated the aspiration of great love and great compassion, one then proceeds to exchange self for other. What this means is that one cultivates the intention that all one's own happiness and causes of happiness (wholesome actions) ought to be given to others —we dedicate or transfer them to others. This is a mental act whereby one turns over all of one's happiness and all of one's causes of happiness to all living beings. Similarly, one wishes that all the suffering and the causes of suffering of all sentient beings accrue to oneself. It has been made very clear in the tradition that this practice will not literally result in the transfer of all of one's happiness and causes of happiness to sentient beings nor will it literally result in the assumption of the suffering and causes of their suffering by oneself. But the meditation of this attitude of exchanging self for other will finally dissolve the barrier between self and other. This meditation will go a long way towards achieving that universal vision which indistinguishably unites self and other in the universal aspiration to be happy and to be free from suffering. So, in a sense, by exchanging self and other we then make the striving of all sentient beings to be happy our own striving to be happy, and similarly we make the striving of all sentient beings to be free from suffering our own wish to be free from suffering.

LOVE AND COMPASSION IN DAILY LIFE

Love and compassion are not meant to be cultivated only in formal meditation. They are also meant to affect the way that we behave in daily life. The application of love and compassion in our daily life implies that we try to save the lives of living beings whenever possible. This means not only saving the lives of human beings but also the lives of animals and insects. I happened to talk to a couple about Buddhist values. The wife, who is a European, has for a long time been interested in Buddhist values. Although the husband, who is Japanese, has an intimate involvement in Buddhist culture, he is not overly involved in Buddhist studies. Yet he made a significant remark. He said that he had seen many Europeans who spent a lot of time studying Buddhism and yet they would not hesitate to kill an insect which happens to come within their reach. Whereas he, like many Japanese who know very little of the technicalities of Buddhism, would not do that. By some means, they will take the insect and throw it out of the window. They would not kill the insect. This does not mean that there will never be occasions when it is necessary to kill because of the need for prevention of disease, for example. But what it means is that we ought to try to avoid taking the life of sentient beings. We should save the lives of the sentient beings whenever possible. Give food, clothing and shelter to the needy. Be friends to the friendless. In this way we implement the ideals of love and compassion in our daily life. One can make love and compassion something which is more than an abstract ideal cultivated within a formalized and isolated context.

MEDITATION ON LOVE AND COMPASSION

In order to meditate on love and compassion, we begin as usual with the refuge and we go on to use the techniques which I talked about beginning with one's mother and then extending the feeling to other sentient beings in a progressive way. One then concludes one's meditation with a dedication of merit.

V. THE ENLIGHTENMENT THOUGHT

We have come to the heart of the practice of the Bodhisattva. And that is the awakening of the thought of enlightenment and the progress one makes towards the enlightenment mind.

AWAKENING THE ENLIGHTENMENT THOUGHT

The awakening of the enlightenment thought is the resolve to achieve enlightenment which is born out of one's altruistic wish for all living beings to be happy and to be free from suffering and the recognition that at this moment we are unable to achieve this goal. There is a juxtaposition between one's cultivation of love and compassion and the recognition of the reality of the present situation—that is we cannot even achieve our own happiness and freedom from suffering let alone achieve the happiness and freedom from suffering of all living beings. One realizes that only through becoming a Buddha oneself can one acquire the ability to secure permanent freedom and happiness for all living beings.

But, for this thought of enlightenment to arise in the mind, one has to erode and weaken the idea of self. One does this in part through the techniques we discussed previously—the cultivation of the equality of self and others, etc. One also does this through recognizing that the self is the source of all our suffering. It is said that the self is the root of the tree of samsara. It is like a stake that fixes us to the cycle of birth and death. The self is like a noose that binds us to the cycle of birth and death. In this context, no matter how much one practices virtuous actions and meditation, one will not be able to escape the cycle of birth and death. He is like a bird bound by a rope—although bound so loosely that he can fly some way. Seeing that a particular idea is a source of pain, why not abandon it? If we were to see that fire is the source of pain, we would stay away from fire so that we will not be burned. Similarly, seeing that the self is the source of all suffering, we should abandon the sense of self. Through cultivating the equality of self and others, the altruistic wish for all sentient beings to be happy and to be free from suffering, and through exchanging self for others, one arrives at the inclination to give priority to the interest of others which is the primary orientation of the Mahayana, the resolve to achieve enlightenment not only for one's own sake but for the sake of all sentient beings.

In the career of the Buddha Sakyamuni, the first awakening of the enlightenment thought took place many aeons ago. In that lifetime, the Buddha was a merchant who had a blind mother. The merchant had to go on a journey to a distant land. As he was the only one available to look after his mother, he was determined to take her along with him so that she would not be left alone at home. The ship that they were sailing in was wrecked as the result of a storm. The Bodhisattva found himself in the water along with the other passengers. Finding himself in that situation, he began to look for his mother, wishing to save her from drowning. Eventually he rescued his mother. At that moment, there arose in his mind the idea of saving all sentient beings from the suffering of samsara.

In this story, we can see some compelling

symbolism, which are later used in the meditational practices for the awakening of the enlightenment thought. The first symbol is the relationship between mother and son, a relationship which is a very close one. As we saw in the last chapter, we begin our cultivation of love and compassion with a consideration of the situation of our mother. The blindness of the mother is a symbol of spiritual blindness, the inability to see the truth, and the ocean is a symbol of samsara.

There are other accounts of the awakening of the enlightenment thought by others on the way to becoming a Buddha. For example, there is the story of the Bodhisattva who was reborn in the realm of the hells because of his misdeeds. There he was yoked to another inmate and was required to draw a cart driven by a warden of the hells. It so happened that the Bodhisattva was more capable in pulling the cart than his companion. As a result, his companion was not able to pull the cart efficiently, which resulted in a beating by the warden. The Bodhisattva asked the warden not to beat his companion since he was too weak but to beat him instead. This wish to relieve his companion of the suffering was the awakening of the enlightenment thought.

THE GOAL OF AWAKENING THE ENLIGHTENMENT THOUGHT

The goal of the career of the Bodhisattva is the attainment of nirvana (freedom) or Bodhi (enlightenment). Freedom and enlightenment are really two names for the same transformed mode of experience. Nirvana expresses the emotive aspect of that transformed experience in that nirvana is essentially liberation from suffering, freedom from the three negative emotions—greed, anger and delusion. Enlightenment on the other hand is a description that has to do with knowledge, the state of one's cognition, in that sense, we talk about enlightenment as being right understanding, as seeing things as they really are, as having omniscience. In both these cases, whether we talk in emotive terms or in poetic terms, there are degrees of emotive freedom and degrees of enlightenment. Essentially, we are here dealing with two kinds of nirvana and Bodhi— the nirvana and the Bodhi of the Arhats, and the nirvana and Bodhi of the Buddhas and Bodhisattvas. This is really again a question of freedom from and freedom to, a question of degrees of enlightenment.

In the case of the Arhat, we have a figure who achieves freedom from the cycle of birth and death for himself, but not freedom to help all other sentient beings. On the other hand, the Buddhas and Bodhisattvas achieve freedom from suffering and rebirth and also freedom to help others. One may say that freedom from aversion to samsara, a freedom to operate in the world of samsara to help others. In the case of the Arhat, there is a degree of insight into the real nature of things, into the three universal marks of existence—impermanence, suffering and not-self, but there is the absence of the omniscience of Buddhahood, for obviously in order to help all beings to achieve emancipation one has to have a clear perception of the situation of all living beings.

Buddhahood implies the nirvana of the Buddha and the enlightenment of the Buddha. It implies a nirvana which is non-abiding. The non-abiding nirvana of the Buddha means that he is not fixed in a transcendental domain because of his altruistic wish to free all sentient beings from suffering. On the other hand, because of his wisdom, he does not abide in the phenomenal realm (samsara) either. He is not bound to samsara. This is the non-abiding nirvana of the advanced Buddhas and advanced Bodhisattvas, which is the goal of the enlightenment thought.

BENEFITS OF AWAKENING THE ENLIGHTENMENT THOUGHT

The awakening of the enlightenment thought is credited with immense benefits by the Mahayana tradition. It is said for example that by the mere awakening of the enlightenment thought a wretch in a prison becomes totally transformed. He becomes a son of the Buddha. He is reborn in the family of the Buddhas because through the awakening of the enlightenment thought he appropriates the character of the Buddhas and Bodhisattvas. Again, it is said that the awakening of the enlightenment thought is like a philosophers stone in that like a philosophers stone which turns base objects into gold, the enlightenment thought turns all sentient beings into Buddhas and Bodhisattvas, transforms all situations into golden situations, and this is because there is no thought within the limits of the mundane world that equals the thought of enlightenment. For example, a person who resolves to give alms to the poor is considered worthy and meritorious even though the alms relieve the suffering of hunger only for a short period. A person who resolves to become a physician to cure physical illness is also a meritorious person. But despite the dedicated effort of his skill he can only save the lives of others for a limited period, he can only mitigate the suffering of others. All these worthy and meritorious resolves and actions are only the smallest fraction of what we have in the awakening of the enlightenment thought because none of these can compare in scope and in quality with the resolve to achieve enlightenment for all living beings. While a physician can relieve the suffering of only a few, the resolve to achieve enlightenment for the benefit of all sentient beings is oriented towards the happiness of all living beings without exception. So the scope of the enlightenment thought is greater. Again, the physician can relieve suffering for a limited period of time only while the resolve to achieve enlightenment implies the aspiration to permanently free all sentient beings from suffering. In this sense, no aspiration is comparable to the enlightenment thought.

The enlightenment thought is also liken to a wish-fulfilling tree—a tree that will grant whatever one wishes, because the uplifting power of that force is such as to provide whatever one wishes. Again, the enlightenment thought is like a friend in that no matter how difficult the circumstances in which we find ourselves, so long as we hold on to the enlightenment thought, we will not succumb to despair. The enlightenment thought is like a refuge or a powerful protector for the frightened, because this thought is unlike any other thought in its scope and quality. It neutralizes the negative karma because of its power which is born of the genuine resolve to achieve Buddhahood for the sake of all living beings.

ASPIRING AND APPLIED ENLIGHTENMENT THOUGHTS

The enlightenment thought can be divided into the aspiring enlightenment thought and the applied enlightenment thought. Thus far, we have considered exclusively the aspirational dimension of the enlightenment thought, the mere wish to achieve enlightenment. This can be likened to the formulation of a plan for a journey. For example, we may decide to spend our holiday in a certain country. We would begin to look into what we have to do in order to travel to that place. We might collect brochures and talk to friends who have been to that place, etc. This constitutes planning. In the same way, having awakened the thought of enlightenment, we might look about for the means of achieving this goal. Just as if we were to find a jewel in a rubbish heap we would be overjoyed to have found a jewel, similarly, having awakened the thought of enlightenment we experience happiness, joy and a sense of transformation. But having found the jewel will not be sufficient. We will want to put the jewel to use. In the same way, the mere aspiration to achieve Buddhahood is not enough. It has to be coupled with the actual application of the enlightenment thought, the practice of the career of the Bodhisattva. This is the applied enlightenment thought, the practice of the path of the Bodhisattva.

CONVENTIONAL AND ULTIMATE ENLIGHTENMENT THOUGHTS

The enlightenment thought can also be divided into the conventional and the ultimate enlightenment thoughts. This division mirrors the division that we have in Buddhism in terms of two levels of truth, the conventional (apparitional) level of reality and the ultimate level of reality. If we look at these two levels of reality in the earlier scholastic tradition, in the Abhidharma tradition, we find that the division between the conventional and the ultimate reality hinges upon the notion of individuals, objects, possessions, etc. So that when we speak of I, my, possession, we are in the realm of convention and when we speak of processes, phenomena (when we have no illusion regarding the existence of ego substances and the substantive relationship between ego and object) we are in the realm of the ultimate reality. This involves a kind of shift of perspective from the perspective of the man in the street to the perspective of the meditator. In the Mahayana, this conception is expanded so that on the conventional level we speak of individuals, self, substances and even of phenomena, on the ultimate level we speak of emptiness, of non-duality.

This particular idea of the conventional and the ultimate reality has its application in the area of the enlightenment thought because so long as we have the dualistic conception of self and other, unenlightened and enlightened existence, the existence of an ordinary being and the existence of a Buddha, we are operating in the realm of the conventional enlightenment thought. Here, of course, it is appropriate to speak of the resolve to attain enlightenment because we still operate in a dualistic frame of reference wherein we have to effect some kind of change in order to achieve Buddhahood. The ultimate enlightenment thought is the mind of the Buddha. It is a mind where there is no self, no phenomena, no mind. There is only emptiness, a transcendence of the extremes or alternatives. We have in the enlightenment mind an experience which can only be described as an integration of emptiness and luminosity. This is the ultimate truth beyond all dualities, beyond self, mind, substance, and phenomena. You will notice that here I am using enlightened thought for the conventional Bodhicitta and the enlightenment mind for the ultimate Bodhicitta. This is because the Sanskrit word 'citta' can be rendered either in a self-contained sense or in an intentional sense. So long as we are talking about the aspiration to achieve enlightenment, we can best render Bodhicitta as the enlightenment thought. But when we have achieved Buddhahood, we then have no aspiration to achieve anything.

Our altruistic activity for the benefit of living beings flows out of the enlightenment mind spontaneously.

THE SIX PERFECTIONS

The path that is to be followed for transforming the enlightenment thought into the enlightenment mind is the path of the six perfections. This is why the Mahayana is sometimes called the Paramitayana, the vehicle of perfections.

The term Paramita, ordinarily translated as perfections, is akin to our English words parameter and metre. It implies limit or measurement. This idea of perfection is the transcendence of a limit, of going beyond a limit. So when we talk about the practice of the perfections, we are actually talking about going beyond the practice of the perfections. We need to keep this in mind because otherwise there is a danger that we will think of the perfections as something static, and the conception of Paramita is a dynamic concept. It entails going beyond itself. In place of the perfection of generosity for instance, we might well say the transcendence of generosity. This is what we mean by Paramita.

The six basic Paramitas are generosity, morality, patience, energy, meditation and wisdom. Those of you who are familiar with other schemes of Buddhist practices will see that there is very little that is new in these practices. The perfections are an important element in the path taught by the Buddha according to all the traditions, whether Theravada or Mahayana. What is new about the six perfections is the way in which they are practiced.

You will recall the therapeutic functions of various components in the Buddhist tradition of mental development. In the context of the perfections, there is no exception to this rule. We can see the perfections as the corrective therapy for particular problems. The perfection of generosity is an antidote to avarice or miserliness, perfection of morality to unwholesome actions, the perfection of patience to anger, the perfection of energy to laziness, the perfection of meditation to distraction and the perfection of wisdom to delusion.

FOUR ADDITIONAL PERFECTIONS

In addition to the six basic perfections, there are four additional perfections—the perfection of skill-in-means, resolution, power and knowledge. These four additional perfections constitute the soteriological capability of the Buddha, the capability to emancipate others. This is perhaps more clearly illustrated in the perfection of skill-in-means because through this perfection the Buddhas and Bodhisattvas are able to develop devices and techniques which are particularly suited to the particular capacity and need of sentient beings.

The perfection of resolution implies the resolution of the Buddhas and Bodhisattvas to emancipate all sentient beings. Power implies the capacity of the Buddhas and Bodhisattvas to implement their resolve—to apply the clear perception of the situation of all living beings. This knowledge is to be differentiated from wisdom. Wisdom in the context of the perfection is insight, whereas here knowledge includes mundane knowledge, knowledge of the sciences, knowledge of the particular mentality of sentient beings so that the emancipating soteriological functions of the enlightened ones can be carried out with the greatest efficiency.

PERFECTION OF WISDOM

Let us look particularly at the perfection of wisdom because this has a very special role to play in the context of the perfections. It is said that the perfection of wisdom is the mother of the Buddhas because all the Buddhas arise out of the perfection of wisdom. Similarly, the perfection of wisdom is like the baking of a clay jar. If we fashion a jar out of clay and leave it unbaked, the jar can be easily shattered. But if we have baked the jar, it will not easily shatter. In the same way, the Bodhisattva who does not practice perfection of wisdom can be easily shattered. His progress towards Buddhahood is not stable. But through the perfection of wisdom, he becomes unshakable. From these two analogies, we can see that the perfection of wisdom has a special role. Again, it is said that the other five perfections are like blind men. No matter how many blind men there are, they cannot on their own reach their goal. But with the help of a single sighted guide, all the five blind men can safely reach their goal. Similarly, without the perfection of wisdom the other perfections cannot reach the goal of Buddhahood.

All these are said because it is the perfection of wisdom that turns all the other perfections into perfections. In other words, generosity is not a perfection without the perfection of wisdom. Why should this be so? What does the perfection of wisdom imply? We have said that ignorance is the idea of self and other, the notion of the separation of self and others—the dichotomy between subject and self. At the heart of this is the notion of a real essence, the essence of subjective existence (self) and the essence of objective existence (phenomena). This notion of independent, inherent existence is common to both the subjective and objective aspects of ignorance.

The perfection of wisdom is the understanding that there exists no independent existing self or object. We have talked about the idea of not-self, the analysis of the personality into its component parts—into the physical and mental components. This is an analytical investigation of the personality. We then proceed with a similar analytical investigation of objects. We can see, for example, that the table before me is not a unitary whole. It is composed of parts—the top, the legs and the screws that hold them together, etc. We can use this analytical approach to refute the idea of an independent existence in sentient beings and in phenomena.

But the analytical approach can only take us so far because this approach leaves us with smaller and smaller bits and pieces of reality, and there is an irresistible temptation to then invest those bits and pieces of reality with that kind of inherent independent existence which we originally invested in the personality and in phenomena. We can see this tendency very clearly in the development of mechanistic, atomistic and reductionist views both in the East and West. The result of the analytical process more often than not is a reduction of reality into its component parts, into atoms, into particular components of mental or physical existence.

The perfection of wisdom is not exclusively about analysis. It is about transcending the analytical way of investigation. What the perfection of wisdom does is to ask us to go beyond mere analysis and to couple analysis with a relational, synthetic form of understanding. We now look at things not merely in terms of their component parts but in terms of their relation, their dependence upon other components. In a sense, we have the notions of wisdom and the perfection of wisdom, analysis being characteristic of wisdom and relation being characteristic of the perfection of wisdom. We have a kind of movement from an analytical mode of investigation to a synthetical mode of investigation.

It is the perfection of wisdom that turns the other perfections into perfections. In what way? It makes them transcendental. It frees them from limitations. We can see that in any kind of action, we have three components — the subject of an action (subjective component), the agent of an action (objective component) and the action itself. The understanding of the perfection of wisdom, when applied to the practice of the perfections, results in the three pure circles. The three pure circles refer to these three components of action—the subject, the object and the action itself. So when we apply our understanding of the perfection of wisdom to the practice of generosity, for example, we realize that the agent of the action is empty. In other words, the giver, the object and the action have no independent intrinsic existence. Thus, no matter what we do, whether we observe the rules of good conduct, the practice of patience, meditation, etc., we are aware of the three pure circles. So for example, as you sit in a lecture, you are aware of the emptiness of the listener, the teaching and the action of listening. I am also aware of the emptiness of the teacher, the objects of the teaching and the action of the teaching. It is this awareness of the emptiness of this subject, object and action that turns the five perfections into perfections. If emptiness were not present, they would not be perfections. They would be ordinary meritorious actions. They would lead to fortunate rebirth, prosperity and progress, etc., but they would not turn our ordinary dualistic mind of ours into the mind of the Buddha. They would not turn our experience into the enlightenment mind of Buddhahood because they would be actions still operating within the framework of subject/object duality, the conception of independently existing things. Done in that way, generosity would only lead to prosperity, morality to well-being, patience to radiance, energy to matter, meditation to peace, and wisdom to freedom from, but not to freedom to. But, if we couple the practice of the perfections with the perfection of wisdom, generosity, morality, patience, energy, meditation and wisdom will lead to Buddhahood. This is the special role of the perfection of wisdom in the context of the perfections. It turns what would otherwise be ordinary meritorious actions that lead to fortunate consequences in this and in future lives into transcendental actions that lead to emancipation.

SKILL-IN-MEANS

Skill-in-means is born of compassion and compassion follows naturally upon wisdom. It is the spontaneous expression of wisdom. We said previously that objectless compassion brought us to the threshold of insight. We said that suffering, sentient beings, phenomena in general, do not exist in reality. We said that this wisdom of emptiness does not imply a turning away from the suffering of sentient beings. So the wisdom of emptiness implies compassion. This of course happens spontaneously because one has been programmed for this reaction through one's careful and exhaustive cultivation of love and compassion, through one's deliberate erosion of the distinction between self and others. It is because we have preceded our cultivation of the perfection of wisdom that wisdom is now automatically coupled with an altruistic concern to free other sentient beings from suffering. It is out of this compassion that skill-in-means is born. This is because compassion requires a variety of devices in order to bring about the emancipation of sentient beings.

The classical expression of skill-in-means is found in the Lotus Sutra (Saddharmapundarika Sutra). In that text, the Buddha likens the three traditions in Buddhism — the Hinayana, the Pratyeka Buddhayana and the Mahayana to so many skilful means. We can see this as a direct answer to the question as to why we have the diversities within the Buddhist tradition—Zen, Theravada, Vajrayana, etc. The Buddha has answered this very directly and explicitly in the parable of the carts. Suppose there was a rich man who lived in a decrepit house, and suppose he had many children. Suppose the children were one day engrossed in their games, occupied with their toys. Suppose that the father were to see that the house had caught fire, knowing that the house was an ancient and decrepit house, the father would be most anxious to get his children out of the house as quickly as possible. So he would call to his children that the house was on fire. But because the children might not know the implication of the fire, they would continue with their games. The father would think that if he were to carry his children bodily, he would not be able to save all his children. So he would think of an expedient device. He would know the inclinations of his children. He would know what attracted them. So he would call to them "Children, I have brought you toys. Outside the house, there are deer carts, bullock carts, goat carts." Responding to his incentive, the children would abandon their games and having come out of the house would find that the father had only the same very fine cart for each and all of them, not different carts.

This parable expresses the Buddhas and Bodhisattvas use of the various methods for bringing about the emancipation of differing sentient beings. In the parable, the rich man is the Buddha. The children are the men of the world who are preoccupied with their activities and distractions, the house is the world, the fire is the fire of greed, anger and delusion, the three kinds of carts are the three vehicles (Sravakayana, Pratyeka Buddhayana and the Bodhisattvayana). When the children came out of the house, the father gave them one cart, the vehicle of Buddhahood. The message is clear. The various traditions—Theravada, Mahayana and Vajrayana, etc.— are just so many devices calculated to suit the particular needs of sentient beings. Once sentient beings have embarked on these vehicles, they will all achieve the same goal of Buddhahood.

This is of course in perfect harmony with the importance of the therapeutic model in Buddhism. The end of the therapy is cure. The therapy along the road to cure differs according to different complaints. We would treat an infection with penicillin, but we would treat psychosomatic illness with psychotherapy. In this same way, there are various treatments for various complaints.

The idea of skill-in-means has contributed to the active encouragement of diversity in the Buddhist tradition. We have a similar idea in the Hindu tradition where we also have a great proliferation of means to the goal. In Buddhism, the idea of skill-in-means is responsible not only for the whole gamut of traditions but also for the whole gamut of practices within each tradition. For example, in the Theravada tradition, we have a division of the personality into six types, so that topics of meditation may he assigned according to their inclinations. For a person with a lustful disposition, one might recommend meditation on the impurities of the body or meditation on death. For those of a devotional character, one might recommend meditation on the Triple Gem. In the Theravada tradition, too, there is the conception of the Buddha's skill-in-means. That is why we find the Buddha speaking in some instances of the need to discipline the self to achieve heaven, happiness and prosperity, and in other places speaking of not-self, and emptiness. These are all expressions of skill-in-means. They are a recognition of the differing capacities of all sentient beings. Not all sentient beings will respond to the same teaching. You can see this at work in Buddhism as a living tradition. For example, you will find that some members of the older generation are happy to go to a temple to do chanting or to offer incense, etc. For them, this is a practice which is compatible to their orientation. If you confront them with an explanation of the doctrines of not-self and emptiness, for example, they will find it very difficult to absorb. In the same way, all these practices are in a way carefully tuned to the needs of sentient beings. There is a danger of thinking the working of skill-in-means as a premeditated kind of operation. It is not that. It is a spontaneous action which is born out of the cultivation of the basic perfections which is enhanced by the perfections of resolution, power and knowledge.

The interdependence between the ordinary sentient beings and the Buddhas and Bodhisattvas is liken to the interdependence between a wind and the wind chime. If we hang a wind chime in the doorway, the chime will give off sounds according to the way in which the wind strikes it. In the same way, having this whole panoply of equipment gained through the practice of the perfections, having wisdom, compassion, skill-in-means, knowledge and power, the enlightened beings respond to the karma of sentient beings. They respond automatically to the winds of the karmic energy of the sentient beings each according to their needs so as to provide just exactly the right techniques to enlightenment.

The idea of skill-in-means is very important in the Mahayana and we can see it operating in many ways. It is in part responsible for the notion in the Mahayana of the appearance of Buddhas and the Bodhisattvas in all kinds of unlikely and unexpected places. We find in Mahayana literature many examples of Buddhas and Bodhisattvas turning up in brothels and gambling dens. This is because the work of emancipation cannot always and only be carried out from the security of conventionally pure or safe havens. A drunkard might very well avoid an overtly spiritual person and yet might be influenced by the words of his companion at drink.

FOUR ARTICLES OF COLLECTION

In addition to the four additional perfections, there are the four articles of collection (Sangani Vastuni) which the Bodhisattva is encouraged to practice. These are adjuncts to the soteriological perfections. The first of these is really an extension of the idea of the perfection of generosity. It is giving and it implies not only the giving of material objects but also the giving of support, encouragement and time, etc.

The practice of giving therefore does not only imply the giving of material objects. This is the first of the four articles of collection that the Bodhisattva is encouraged to practice. The second is pleasant speech. This is an aid to the Bodhisattva in his work of emancipation. If he is to have an effect on others, he must have pleasant speech. The third is empathy. It is the capacity to share the happiness and suffering of others, to identify with them. The last is consistency and harmony between actions and words. The precepts that he teaches must be exemplified in his own life.

As you look back at the practices enjoined for the Bodhisattva—the six basic perfections, the four additional perfections and the four articles of collection—you will see that the life of the layman is particularly well suited to the practice of the Bodhisattva path. That is why if you look at the legendary accounts of the Bodhisattvas in the Jataka literature, you will find that most of the Bodhisattvas are laymen. That is why in the Mahayana we find that the lay life achieves a parity with the monastic life as a vehicle for achieving the highest goal, though there is no rejection of the monastic system. In many ways, the lay life is more conducive to practice the perfections of the Bodhisattva than is the monastic life. A layman has more opportunities to practice the perfection of generosity, morality, and patience than a monk. The same is true of the four articles of collection. All of them can be practiced in the context of the lay life. In the Mahayana, the life of the layman and laywoman comes into its own. It achieves equal status with the monastic life. In some ways it almost supersedes the monastic life as the prime vehicle for achieving Buddhahood.

MEDITATION ON AWAKENING THE ENLIGHTENMENT THOUGHT

In the context of structured meditation on the enlightenment thought, we begin with the recitation of the refuge formula. We proceed to a meditation on the awakening of the enlightenment thought. We awaken the enlightenment thought by running through our meditation on love and compassion as described previously. We bring into focus the juxtaposition of the altruistic wish for all living beings to be permanently happy and free from suffering and our current inability to achieve this wish. Having done that, we bring to mind the need to achieve Buddhahood in order to rescue all sentient beings from suffering and to establish them permanently in happiness.

One can enforce the exclusivity of the goal of Buddhahood by running through the comparative inability of other roles and functions to achieve the lasting happiness of all sentient beings. One can run through the limitations of more ordinary resolves to benefit living beings. This includes not only the resolve of physicians, donors, etc., but also the resolve that social workers, political figures, etc., might have to improve the conditions of sentient beings. All of these pale into insignificance beside the resolve to achieve Buddhahood for all sentient beings.

ENLIGHTENMENT THOUGHT IN DAILY LIFE

Even outside the context of structured formal meditation, one ought to recall one's aspiration to achieve Buddhahood. One ought never to relinquish one's aspiration to achieve Buddhahood. As I suggested previously regarding the techniques to transform neutral ineffective actions into meritorious actions, one can forge an intentional link between a particular action and the attainment of enlightenment of all sentient beings, as, for example, when we leave home, we may think, "Just as I leave my home, may all beings set out on the path to enlightenment," and when returning home, "As I return to my home, may all beings achieve enlightenment," etc. We have this also in the formalized context of the meditation in the formula of dedication whereby we dedicate whatever positive energy has been created by the meditation to the achievement of Buddhahood of all living beings. In this way, we hold on to the enlightenment thought no matter where we are, no matter how difficult the situation we find ourselves in.

ACHIEVEMENT OF BUDDHAHOOD

The practice of the six perfections results in the realization of Buddhahood. Buddhahood has two dimensions—the Dharmakaya, which is the transcendental dimension beyond thought and expression, and the Rupakaya, which is the form dimension. The Rupakaya is sub-divided into a terrestrial form body and a celestial form body. The practice of the first three perfections (generosity, morality and patience) results in the acquisition of the Rupakaya, while the practice of the last two perfections (meditation and wisdom) results in the acquisition of the Dharmakaya. Energy, the fourth perfection, is required in both the acquisitions. The union of these two bodies is the being of Buddhahood.

It is the practices of the perfection of meditation and wisdom that leads to the acquisition of the transcendental dimension of Buddhahood. Later, we are going to look at the practices of meditation and wisdom, and how each of them is to be cultivated individually and how they have to be brought together to bring about the acquisition of the transcendental dimension of Buddhahood.

VI. Tranquility

We will discuss a topic which is really at the heart of the Buddhist tradition of mental development, and that is the techniques for developing tranquility or quietude (samatha). The importance of this topic in the Buddhist tradition should not be underestimated, but neither as we shall see later, should it be overestimated.

Importance of Tranquility

The achievement of tranquility, of a concentrated state of mind, is one of the two key components in turning the conventional enlightenment thought into the ultimate enlightenment thought. Tranquility together with insight are key components in achieving the accomplishment of knowledge. We mentioned previously that the perfections are divided into two groups. The first three perfections— giving, good conduct and patience belong to the group which leads to the accumulation of merit. The last two— meditation and wisdom—belong to the group which leads to the accumulation of knowledge. The remaining perfection, energy, is required for both accumulations. The first three perfections are the causes of achieving the phenomenal aspect of Buddhahood (Rupakaya) while the last two perfections are the causes of achieving the transcendental aspect of Buddhahood (Dharmakaya). Thus, in looking at tranquility, we come to the first of the two key components, which are necessary for achieving the transcendental dimension of Buddhahood.

Achieving the transcendental aspect of Buddhahood also means changing the conventional enlightenment thought into the ultimate enlightenment thought, or the enlightenment mind, the mind of a Buddha. The distinction between the conventional and ultimate enlightenment thoughts is really the distinction between an experience that is dualistic and one that is non-dual. At the stage of the conventional enlightenment thought, we have a number of dualities to deal with. There is the duality between an unenlightened experience and an enlightened experience. We conceive of ourselves as being in an unenlightened condition and as having to strive for enlightenment. We also conceive of ourselves and other sentient beings as being different. We conceive of having to save other sentient beings from suffering, etc. But, on the stage of the ultimate enlightenment mind, all dualities cease to exist.

A commonly used metaphor for this transition from the conventional enlightenment thought to the ultimate enlightenment thought is that of dream and awakening. A virgin girl may dream that she has given birth to a child, and then she may dream that the child had died. She will first experience happiness, and then suffering. However, when she awakens, she will realize that neither was the child born, nor did it die. In the same way, in the unenlightened condition, all phenomena, all experiences, are characterized by birth and death, by arising and destruction. But on the enlightened stage, it is seen that all phenomena never really arose, nor did they really die. The Buddha said that there is an unborn and an undying. This unborn and undying, which is the goal of the Buddhist path, is not something which is anywhere else. The realization of this does not imply any movement or travel to another location. It is a subjective change, a change in the way we see things. When one awakens from a dream, the objects and impressions of the dream do not really go anywhere. In order to make this change in one's mind, from the conventional dualistic point of view to the enlightened mind, the main practices that one must perfect are the practices of tranquility and insight.

THE THREE STEPS OF MENTAL DEVELOPMENT

In the Buddhist tradition, mental development is not merely a case of sitting cross-legged before an image, or in a temple. It is not merely a question of observing the processes of inhalation and exhalation of the breath. It is something which has to be integrated into our lives, which has to be applied to every moment of our existence, to every conscious action. This is reflected in the Buddhist emphasis on the importance of the mind in shaping the nature of our experience, how the mind colors and determines the nature of our experience. It is also reflected, in a more specific way, in the three steps of the eight-fold path that belong to the mental development group. These three steps are right effort, right mindfulness and right meditation. Only the third of these, that is meditation, can in any way be described as formal, structured sitting meditation. Effort and mindfulness are components which have to be practiced in all kinds of unstructured, free situations.

1 *Right Effort*

In general, right effort means having an energetic and enthusiastic approach to one's tasks and activities. It has been said that to practice right effort, one has to emulate the feeling of an elephant which enters a pool of cool water during the heat of the mid-day sun or one might say the feeling when we enter an air-conditioned room after we have been out in the noon-day sun. We will be enthusiastic about entering the delicious coldness of the room. In the same way, right effort should be expressed as an enthusiastic response to the task that we undertake. Let us therefore be clear about what right effort is not. It is not a plodding, dogged, stolid pursuit of our objectives. Rather, it is an energetic and positive approach to our tasks.

There is another caution in regard to right effort. It should not result in tension, in an agitated or excited state of mind. Right effort should be a balanced attitude which combines maximum or optimum alertness with maximum or optimum relaxation because right effort is that kind of equipoise that combines alertness with relaxation. There was a well-known Tibetan yogini who used to say to her students, "Alert, alert! Relax, relax!" Just as it is the string which is not too tight and not too loose that will produce the most harmonious sound, in the same way right effort is the tuning of the mind in such a way that it is not too tense and not too slack.

Specifically, in the Buddhist tradition, right effort is applied in four ways. These are the effort to prevent unwholesome thoughts from arising, the effort to abandon such unwholesome thoughts once they have arisen, the effort to cultivate wholesome thoughts (thoughts that are free from greed, anger and delusion), and the effort to maintain and conserve these thoughts once they have arisen. You will see that these four right efforts apply to our mental activities, to the condition of our mind during all conscious states.

This emphasis that the Buddha placed upon right effort is completely consistent with his emphasis upon the individual as the one who is responsible for, and who determines, his destiny. There were, in the Buddha's time, as there are now, other views about the forces that shape and determine man's destiny. One prevalent view was that man's destiny was determined by impersonal forces, by fate. There was a teacher (Makkhali Gosala) who taught that liberation would occur at a preordained moment. On the other hand, there were others who belong to the sacrificial religion of the Vedas, who were schools of thought that believed in grace, in a superior being who could grant salvation. In either of these views, one must rely upon a power outside of one's self for attaining liberation. The Buddha rejected such ideas and placed the responsibility for freedom or for bondage in the cycle of birth and death squarely on the shoulders of the individual. His emphasis on the need for energy, effort and endeavor is evidence of this. A good indication of the importance that the Buddha placed on right effort, right mindfulness and right meditation is found in the thirty-seven practices conducive to attaining enlightenment. These practices are important in all the Buddhist traditions. They were taught by the Buddha not long before he entered into final nirvana, which is another indication of the importance that he placed on them. If we look at these thirty-seven practices, we see that more than half of them are concerned with energy, endeavor, effort, mindfulness and meditation.

2 Right Mindfulness

The next factor of the eight-fold path that belongs to the mental development group is mindfulness. Mindfulness is a reflective awareness of one's situation, of one's actions, words and thoughts. The Buddha said that the mind is the root, the source, of all good qualities. He also called mindfulness, "The one way to freedom from suffering, the one way to enlightenment." The Buddha placed this emphasis on mindfulness because it is awareness that brings about a redirection in one's life, in one's development. In the absence of mindfulness, all of us behave very much like cogs in a machine. Most people are familiar with the psychological work of Pavlov, and the fact that his dogs would salivate upon hearing the footsteps of their keeper, the one who fed them. This is the beginning of the principle of conditioned response: the principle that teaches that one responds to stimuli in an automatic, mechanical determined way. This model is not very far wrong if we consider the ordinary, unmindful behavior of many of us. But this can be changed by becoming aware of one's situation.

That is why it has been said that, when you are walking, Buddhism means not to stumble. When you are driving a car, Buddhism means not to have an accident. When you are making a cup of tea, Buddhism means to make it well. Be aware of what you are doing. Do not let your mind wander. This happens to all of us. As you are talking to someone, your mind may be on something that happened a few hours before or it may be racing ahead to something that you anticipate might happen in the future. Our minds are very seldom precisely on what we are doing. They are here, and there, and everywhere. This can only diminish efficiency. Here we have a very practical application of mindfulness. If one wanted to increase one's productivity and efficiency, one should practice mindfulness, because certainly if one's mind is on what one is doing, one will do it more efficiently.

The cultivation of mindfulness can turn one's life around in a very specific and dramatic way. This was indicated by the Buddha when he said that mindfulness is the source of life and mindlessness is the source of death. One can interpret this in a very prosaic and mundane way by saying that if one is not mindful while crossing the street one might end up dead. But what the Buddha meant is that mindfulness is the cause of nirvana whereas mindlessness is the cause of repeated birth and death in the cycle of samsara.

The Buddha and other Buddhist teachers have cited examples of individuals who have changed their lives through the practice of mindfulness. Nanda the Buddha's half brother, was obsessed with sensuality. Yet, through mindfulness, he was able to control his obsession and became known as the foremost in the control of his senses. Similarly, Angulimala turned his life around through the practice of mindfulness.

Mindfulness is particularly important because the Buddhist tradition teaches that the mind is the most precious possession that we have. In the more developed phases of Buddhism—the Mahayana and Vajrayana—the mind is likened to a wish-fulfilling gem, because the mind can give us either nirvana or samsara. The mind is the root of the cycle of birth and death, and it is also the root of enlightenment. The mind is also liken to a crystal, if you put a crystal before a red background, the crystal will appear red, if you put the crystal before a blue background, it will appear blue. The mind is like that. If it is influenced by the afflictions—greed, anger and delusion—then samsara will appear, if the mind is influenced by the opposites—that is by non-greed, non-anger and non-delusion—then nirvana will appear. The mind is the source of all these things, and therefore is the most precious thing we have.

If the mind is so precious, it stands to reason that one should keep a close watch on it. One will look after it carefully. In the Tibetan tradition, it is said that if one had a fine horse one would keep a close watch on it and take care of it. So it is with the mind, one ought to keep an eye on it and take good care of it.

One should disengage the mind from obsessive involvement in sensual pleasures. This does not mean that one must withdraw oneself from the world of sense-objects. It does not mean that one should figuratively build a wall around oneself, it does not even mean that one should shut one's eyes, plug one's ears or close our nose. The Buddha said that the objects of the senses are like snares, but the practitioner who knows how to avoid becoming entangled in them is like a deer who may lay down on a snare in the forest and yet is not caught in it. He is able to get away. Thus, the idea is not to try to run away from the objects of the senses. Rather, it is to avoid becoming entangled in them. Mindfulness is being aware of the dangers of the entanglements inherent in sensual pleasures and keeping a reign on the mind. Mindfulness enables one to keep the mind from running uncontrollably after stimuli, to keep the mind from reacting in a mechanical way to the stimuli of the senses.

Specifically, the Buddhist tradition speaks of the four applications or stations of mindfulness. This refers to the application of mindfulness with regard to the body, the feelings, the perceptions and the mind itself. This is a systematic and progressive application of the principle of mindfulness to specific areas of personal experience. These specific areas are analogous to the physical and mental factors of personal experience that we have in the teaching of the five aggregates—matter (body and physical objects around us), feeling (emotive component), perception (intellectual component), mental formation (volitional component) and consciousness. The four applications of mindfulness between them exhaust all the various areas of personal experience.

In practical terms, mindfulness is being aware of what one is doing, when one is doing it. For example, when walking, the monk knows that he is walking. When sitting, he knows that he is sitting. When lying down, he knows that he is lying down. When experiencing unwholesome volitions, he is aware of it. Gradually, one can become aware of what one is doing at all times. This practice of mindfulness is something which we can do at all times and in all places. From time to time as one remembers, one can check upon the activity of one's mind. What is your mind doing at this very moment? Is it on what you are doing here and now, or is it somewhere else. This kind of repeated exercise will gradually bring about an awareness that will allow for a creative approach to life, to experience. None of us wants to go through life like Pavlov's dogs, simply responding to stimuli. We would want to have some control over our activities.

3 Right Meditation

Let us look now at the third component of the mental development group, namely meditation or concentration. This is what we think of as formal meditation, focussing the mind upon an object, seeking to gain one-pointedness of mind. This practice of concentrating the mind is a very ancient practice. It goes back at least to the third millennia

BC. This is not surprising since the Buddhist tradition pre-dates the Buddha. This is clear from the Buddha's own statements in which he says that the path that he teaches is an ancient path, the goal that he teaches is an ancient goal. It is supported by the Buddhist tradition of the existence of previous Buddhas. This is further supported by literary and archaeological evidence. For example, in the excavations of some of the major cities of the Indus Valley Civilization, there have been found a number of images of individuals, sitting cross-legged, with their outstretched palms resting on their knees, with their eyes half closed, quite unmistakably in postures of meditation. Yoga, in its general meaning, means to join together. In the context of meditation, it means to unite the mind with an object, to fuse or identify the mind with an object.

Meditation has to be understood in the light of what we said earlier about optimum alertness and optimum relaxation. There has been a lot of mystification of meditation and of meditative states. It is important to realize that although the altered state of meditative consciousness differ from normal consciousness as do certain other altered states of consciousness, they have a particular character which is very different from these other states. This is because the altered state of meditative consciousness avoids the extremes of coma and frenzy, of over-relaxation and over-agitation.

Let us look for a moment at some of these other altered states of consciousness. The hypnotic state is a semi-conscious state, almost an unconscious passive state because the subject can not participate in the therapy. Similarly, dream is a highly relaxed, unstructured and undirected state of consciousness. Even the psychoanalytic state of mind is unstructured because the subject is asked to 'free associate.' On the other hand, we have some states which are characterized by over-excitement, by agitation. This is typical of psychotic states, and some of the drug-induced altered states of consciousness. In contrast, in the meditative state we have optimal alertness with optimal relaxation, an altered state which is different from the other altered states of consciousness. We have an altered state of consciousness which is characterized by calm and clarity.

MEDITATION AND WISDOM

I have mentioned that meditation has a particular place in Buddhism. It has a particular place that ought not to be under-rated nor over-rated. This is also to say something about the special place of meditation within the Buddhist tradition. We know from the accounts of the Buddha's life that in his quest for enlightenment he visited two teachers soon after he left his father's palace and that he learned meditative techniques from them. We find that the meditative states which the aspiring Bodhisattva was able to attain by means of the teachings of these two teachers are exactly parallel to levels of concentration that are taught in Buddhism. In Buddhism, we normally speak of four or five form-sphere meditations in which the mind becomes one-pointed, but in which it is still oriented toward objects that are material, that have form. Then, we speak of four formless sphere meditations wherein the objects toward which the meditative consciousness is directed are formless, such as the infinity of space, the infinity of consciousness and so forth. The aspiring Bodhisattva achieved all of these meditative states under the tutelage of these two teachers. Yet he left these two teachers to seek further. He went on to follow the path of austerities. When he finally returned to meditation, it was with a difference. This is the key to an understanding of the place of meditation within the Buddhist tradition. The ultimate achievement in the yogic tradition is the attainment of this highly concentrated state of consciousness oriented towards an immaterial object, a formless state of concentration. This achievement is not the goal in Buddhism because according to the Buddha, although meditation can lead one to the pinnacle of samsara, it cannot free one unless it is combined with wisdom. Sooner or later, when the power of that meditative absorption is exhausted, one will again re-enter a lower state of existence. Thus, one might say that through practicing meditation alone, one can get to the top of the ferris wheel of samsara, but one cannot get off unless one combines meditation with wisdom. This is what the Buddha did on the night of his enlightenment. He says that on this night, with his mind concentrated and made supple and pure through the practice of meditation, he then directed his mind to the recollection of his former lives, to the perception of the workings of karma, and finally to the causes of suffering and rebirth.

The combining of meditation and wisdom is like the viewing of a painting in a darkened room with the aid of a torch. If the torch is not steady because of a shaky hand, or there are draughts in the room, it will be difficult to see the painting. Similarly, if one wants to see reality clearly, the mind has to be made steady, protected from the draughts of distraction.

Thus, in Buddhism, meditation is instrumental. It is a means to an end and not an end in itself. A lot of Buddhist literature is devoted to some of the pitfalls of practicing meditation by itself without wisdom. What are some of these pitfalls? Meditation without wisdom can lead to the illusion of an ultimate essence, a super-ego, a supreme soul or supreme god. It can lead to craving for repetition of those meditative experiences. It can lead to pride or arrogance. Thus, the point of combining meditation with wisdom, first and foremost, is to avoid getting caught in some kind of super-conscious limbo, from which one will eventually have to emerge and re-enter the cycle of birth and death.

This point of combining meditation with wisdom has been repeated by Buddhist teachers from the Buddha himself right up to the present. Nagarjuna, in the 2nd Century in India, says that without meditation, there is no wisdom; without wisdom, there is no meditation. But for one who combines meditation and wisdom, the whole ocean of samsara is like the water in a cow's hoof-print in the mud after a shower. Hui Neng, the Sixth Patriarch of China, said that wisdom and meditation go together like a lamp and its light.

To gain one-pointedness of mind, which is the object of meditation, it is important to avoid distractions and to avoid attachments. This does not contradict what was said earlier regarding the emphasis upon one's attitude towards objects of the senses rather than the objects of the senses themselves. Obviously if we are going to try to calm the mind down, to get the mind to focus single-pointedly upon a given object, it is important to minimize and, as far as possible, avoid distractions and attachments. We can all see that for example, if we happen to be at work on a report, and we have a television show that we are interested in on at the same time, this is a distraction that will get in the way of concentrating on the report. Similarly, if we happen to be in love or in an argument with someone, this attachment or emotional involvement will get in the way of our concentration. In order that concentration be more easily achieved, it is important to avoid distractions and attachments as much as possible. One good way to do this is to isolate body, voice and mind. This is difficult for most people who hold full-time jobs and have a lot of temporal responsibilities. Nonetheless, it is an extremely effective way to get down to some serious work on meditation, to create a situation even for a few days or for a week, wherein one is isolated from the ordinary distractions and activities that make up our everyday lives. One way in which this is often done in the Buddhist tradition is to have a room to oneself, and to put aside a rather large amount of time each day to devote to meditation, and to refrain from leaving the immediate neighborhood of that place of meditation. Of course, one may go for a walk to relieve the confinement, but one ought not to go downtown and eat an ice cream cone, or see a film, etc. These are the preliminaries, or prerequisites, for really coming to grip with the task of getting control over one's mind.

If you cannot do this at the moment, there is nothing to prevent you from practicing meditation for relatively short periods in the evening or morning in your home. If you are going to do this because you are unable to create a situation of isolation, then you ought to be clear and careful to create propitious and suitable circumstances to meditate within the context of your daily life. The place of one's meditation should be conducive to meditation both physically and mentally. Food, water, shelter and medicine should be readily available and adequate. The place of meditation should be orderly and clean. One's meditation seat should be comfortable and if possible facing a shrine or an image of the Buddha. The place of meditation should be free from distractions, interference and interruption from beings hostile to one's practice. We might add to that the suggestion that one chooses a suitable time for meditation, a quiet time in the house, when one is rested and refreshed. In this context, the early morning, just after arising, is probably one of the better times to practice meditation. This is because one is rested and has a mind which has not been cluttered or agitated by the events of the day. Moreover, this is usually a period when one is not in a slothful state as a result of eating.

Besides creating a situation in which the meditation would have a better chance of success, one point which I would like to emphasize is that it should be undertaken with a happy and relaxed frame of mind. One should not press or push too hard like the overly tight string on a guitar which is likely to break. This is the most common cause of problems in meditation. Do not overdo it. The meditation should not become a stressful experience as this can create a resistance to meditation which will be a great obstacle.

TECHNIQUES FOR ACHIEVING TRANQUILITY

Let us now look specifically at the various techniques used in Buddhism to concentrate the mind. Here again, it will be useful to recall the therapeutic analogy that we have talked about before. One can think about the whole of Buddhist practice as a therapy. This means that we have particular problems, complaints or disorders and we have therapies, correctives and treatments for these problems. Similarly, in the context of meditation, we have obstacles and hindrances, and we have ways of overcoming them.

1 The Theravada Tradition

We will first look at the scheme outlined in the Theravada and Abhidharma traditions and then look at the scheme outlined in the Mahayana tradition. These schemes are not contradictory, though they are slightly different. In the Theravada and Abhidharma traditions, five hindrances or obstacles to concentration are indicated. These are lust or sensual desire, ill will, doubt, sloth and torpor, and agitation and worry. We can see that these five hindrances belong to slightly different categories of experience. For example, sloth and torpor and agitation and worry are, by and large, the emotive category of experience. They have to do with one's feelings, one's attitude. Sloth and torpor is an attitude of indolence, of dullness, of stupor, sleepiness, drowsiness. Agitation and worry is an excited state. In this respect, you will recall that meditation avoids the extremes of other altered states of consciousness—the relaxed state and the agitated state. Then we have what might be called volitional obstacles—desire or lust in the one hand, and ill will on the other. Finally, doubt which is a kind of indecision or vacillation on the part of the mind. This can be called an intellectual hindrance.

We have these five hindrances to concentration, and we have five antidotes which correct and counter these hindrances and thereby make it possible to achieve concentration of mind. These antidotes are called the five factors of concentration or the five intensifying factors. Let us consider them one by one.

With respect to sloth and torpor, we have the corrective of initial application or discursive thought. This means the initial focussing of the mind on an object, or the first placing of the mind upon the object. It is described as striking the object, hitting upon the object, directing the mind towards the object. It is also described as mounting the mind upon the object, in the same way that one would mount a horse. Initial application counters sloth and torpor, the dull, lethargic, drowsy, undirected condition of consciousness.

With respect to doubt, indecision and vacillation of mind we have the corrective of sustained application. This means the exertion of continuous pressure of the mind upon the object so that where initial application is the placing of the mind upon the object, sustained application is keeping the mind mounted, on the object. Just as one who rides a horse needs to apply some pressure in order not to fall from the horse, similarly one would need sustained application in order to keep the mind on the object of concentration.

With respect to ill will and aversion, we have the corrective of interest. By cultivating interest one counters ill will and aversion. What is interest? Interest inspires, interest encourages. It is said that interest is like hearing about a pool of water in an oasis by a man lost in the desert. He would be interested. This is very important in the context of meditation, as sometimes one might experience aversion to the meditation. There will be times when one feels fed up with meditation, with having to sit cross-legged. At this point, one needs to call up interest in the goals of meditation.

With respect to agitation and worry, we have the corrective of happiness, a sense of ease or joy. People who are happy, who are experiencing mental and physical ease, are protected from agitation and worry.

Finally, we have greed, or desire for objects of the senses. The mental factor that corrects this is one-pointedness of mind, the focussing of the mind upon an object. Why?

Because greed or desire for the objects of the senses is a reaching beyond oneself, reaching for something else. As long as the mind is focussed upon an object, greed is corrected because the mind is not seeking out something else.

These are the five factors of concentration—initial application, sustained application, interest, happiness and one-pointedness which correct the five obstacles to concentration. It is important to remember that these five factors are not exclusively found in meditative concentration. They are also found in many ordinary states of consciousness. We ought to be wary of the mystification of meditative experience. Meditation is not a mystery. The factors that contribute to meditative concentration are not a mystery. For example, initial application and sustained application are present in our daily consciousness. They are particularly important in intellectual pursuits. Interest is something that we all know about, if we are interested in something, we stick to it. We usually do well in it. We can even see the crucial importance of interest. All of us have known elderly persons, who slip rapidly into senility and death because once they have retired they have no interests. On the other hand, we have all known old people who have some interests and remain vital, alert and healthy to very old age. Similarly, a child who is interested in his studies will do well. He will not do well if he is not interested. We are all also familiar with happiness. We experience happiness from time to time. Lastly, one might think that surely one-pointedness must belong only to meditative experience. This is not so. Every conscious moment has an element of one-pointedness in it. If one-pointedness were not present in consciousness at all times, we would not be able to pick out an object from other objects. Without the factor of one-pointedness, consciousness would always be an amorphous, diffused continuum. When a single object is picked out from the general undifferentiated stream of experience—as, for example, my voice, an image, a scent, and focussed upon, even for a moment—this is one-pointedness. Of course, when one-pointedness is developed to its ultimate potential, it becomes synonymous with the attainment of supernormal states of concentration.

These five factors can be cultivated for short-term benefits, as well as for long-term benefits. This is something which is characteristic of Buddhism—the presentation of short-term or provisional goals, and of long-term goals. It has been said that the practice of Buddhism at first leads to prosperity and happiness. Ultimately it leads to freedom. Here, too, the practice of concentration may be cultivated initially in order to bring about greater success or efficiency in one's personal or professional life. However, if concentration is developed sufficiently, and combined with wisdom, the five factors of concentration become important elements in the attainment of enlightenment.

2 The Mahayana Tradition

The scheme that we find prevalent in the Theravada and Abhidharma traditions is slightly changed in the Mahayana tradition which we are dealing with. There is no radical difference between the two. What we find in this tradition is a kind of stripping down of the concepts involved. One might say it becomes less loaded. In the Theravada tradition, the five obstacles are very familiar villains, problems like greed and ill will. In the Mahayana description, the factors involved are more technical aspects of the dynamics of achieving mental concentration. What are these five obstacles in the Mahayana tradition? The first is laziness or indolence. This is quite similar to sloth and torpor in the Theravada tradition. The second obstacle is forgetfulness. The third is called "sinking and scattering." One might describe it as stagnation and agitation. The fourth obstacle is failing to apply the therapies. The fifth obstacle is over-applying the therapies.

Let us look at these hindrances in relation to their correctives. The first obstacle, indolence or laziness, is corrected by desire. Some may find it peculiar that here desire functions as a therapeutic device—for after all, in the Theravada scheme, desire is one of the obstacles. We must remember that desire is of two kinds, depending upon the object toward which it is directed. Desire for sensual objects is a constraining, clinging and limiting force. But desire for enlightenment is a liberating force. Desire, like electricity, is merely energy. Its application is all important. Similarly, diligence, energy and effort are correctives to indolence. Faith is also a corrective to indolence because if one can develop faith one can overcome lethargy. The first obstacle of indolence or laziness can be overcome by desire, by diligence or by faith.

The second obstacle, forgetfulness, is overcome by recollection, by mindfulness. Literally, mindfulness means remembering. It corrects forgetfulness. If you are sitting in meditation you are liable to forget why you are meditating, to forget the suffering of all living beings, the kindness of your mother, that all living beings have been your mothers, the specific techniques of meditation, etc. By being mindful of these teachings and instructions, by recollection, we can correct forgetfulness.

The third obstacle, stagnation and agitation, is corrected by watchfulness. This means keeping a watch on what is happening so that you know whether you are sinking into a state of stagnation of semi-consciousness, or whether you are becoming agitated, with your mind jumping all over.

The fourth obstacle is failing to apply the therapy. This is countered by applying the therapy. When you see a problem happening—for example, sinking or scattering—you must apply the appropriate therapy. Similarly, you must guard against the fifth hindrance of over-applying the therapy by equanimity or even-mindedness.

Stagnation and agitation, or sinking and scattering, are two of the most common obstacles to meditative concentration. They are analogous to over-relaxation and over-tension. They are also analogous to the situation of the various states of altered consciousness that we have discussed. There are a number of techniques that are prescribed to counter these problems. These techniques can be applied not only in the context of the mental activity that goes on in the process of meditation, but also in the context of the environment of meditation. In the context of the mental activity of meditation, stagnation can be countered by initial application and interest. Agitation can be countered by happiness and one-pointedness. In the context of the environment of meditation there are also a number of correctives. If one is having trouble with sinking or stagnation, one can correct this by sitting in meditation for shorter periods. Another corrective is to use a higher seat or cushion for meditation. One can also wear lighter clothing. In cool climates, one can open a window to lower the temperature. Another method is to eat less food, if the opposite problem—that is scattering or agitation—arises, you can apply the opposite correctives. Spend longer times in meditation, use a lower seat, eat more, and wear warmer clothing. Thus, one can apply both mental and environmental correctives to these very common and major problems of sinking and scattering.

In the tradition of Asanga and Vasubhandu, the tradition which supplies the foundation of Mahayana meditative techniques and which was handed down to Asanga by the heavenly Bodhisattva Maitreya, there are nine factors of concentration by means of which one-pointed concentration can be achieved. Here again we will notice certain similarities between these and the factors of concentration found in the Theravada tradition. The first two of these nine factors are the same as those of the Theravada tradition: namely, initial application and sustained application. The third factor is called conscious re-settling. We must try to understand these techniques in the context of the meditative experience. Let us try to envisage the meditative experience in our mind's eye. Following initial and sustained placing of the mind upon the object of meditation, the mind will stray from the object unless one is very gifted at creating meditative consciousness. This must be corrected by the third factor suggested here; the technique called conscious re-settling. We realize that our mind has strayed from the object, and we consciously re-settle the mind upon the object. This is followed by the fourth technique, which is to sustain that re-settling of the mind on the object. The fifth technique is referred to as taming the mind, or disciplining of the mind. Here, once the mind has settled upon the object again, there will be a tendency for the mind to rebel against this placement, against this constraint. Thus, the mind must be consciously tamed. The sixth factor is called pacification, and it follows from taming. Pacification means that the rebellious nature of the mind that is initially countered by taming or disciplining, by restraint, is pacified. It is very common in the Buddhist tradition to use the analogy of the taming of an animal to illustrate the process of learning to concentrate the mind in meditation. Taming the mind is analogous to taming a horse. Pacification is the next step in the process, when the animal is no longer rebelling, no longer needs to have a disciplining hand on the reins. The next step, the seventh factor, is called enhanced pacification, and this is when the horse not only is pacified, but he actually begins to feel comfortable in his role, when he actually begins to enjoy going off for a run with someone on his back. At this stage of meditation, the mind is suffused with a sense of well being, a sense of peace. The eighth stage in this process is single-pointed. Once the mind has passed through the previous stages, from initial application to enhanced pacification, it achieves single-pointedness. Finally, the ninth step is the acquisition of effortless single-pointed placing. What was initially a result that could only be achieved through very meticulous practice, and only by very small degrees can now be achieved effortlessly and immediately.

THE FOUR PSYCHIC EXPERIENCES

There is encouragement for everyone who has tried to meditate and found it very difficult. The Tibetan tradition identifies four types of psychic experiences on the way to achieving single-pointed concentration. By looking at these four types of psychic experience, we will understand the stages through which we have to pass in order to develop a concentrated mind. We will be forewarned of these stages, and we will know how to handle them. We will feel familiar and comfortable when these phenomena arise. It is like having a map of a country through which one is going to pass.

The first of these four experiences is likened to a mountain waterfall. A mountain waterfall rushes down. It is tumultuous; it is unrestrained. The first experience we will have when we sit down to meditate will be the experience of the mountain waterfall. We will experience a rush of thoughts, a rush of distractions. One never knew that one had so many thoughts. This is often misinterpreted. People often mistakenly come to the conclusion that meditation has caused an increase in the number of thoughts that they have. This is not the case. As one stirs the water in a bucket, it becomes cloudy as dirt comes to the surface. The dirt was always there, but the act of stirring the water has brought it to the surface. The act of focussing and concentrating the mind has brought all the thoughts and distractions into focus. One notices these thoughts and distractions which went unnoticed previously. Again, suppose two objects are both travelling at the same speed. They will be stationary with respect to each other. If one of the objects slows down or stops, the movement of the other object becomes apparent. Similarly, when the mind becomes even marginally steady, the rush of thoughts becomes more apparent. Do not be discouraged by this experience of the waterfall, as it is a natural consequence of meditation.

The second stage of experience is described as falls and pools. This means that as the ability to concentrate the mind increases there will be periods of calm or tranquility. These periods of tranquility will be interspersed with periods of the waterfall experience when thoughts and distractions rush through the mind.

The third stage of experience is likened to a lake. A lake is generally calm and tranquil. But a lake has rivers and streams entering it at its peripheries. At this stage, one's tranquility and concentration of mind is, in general, central. It becomes almost, but not quite, total. From time to time, a thought will appear at the periphery of the mind, and will be absorbed into the calmness and tranquility at the center of the mind, in the way that the water of a stream is absorbed into a lake. A ripple is created at the periphery, but it is absorbed into the tranquil depths of the lake.

Finally, when one-pointedness is perfectly achieved, we reach the fourth stage where our experience may be likened to a waveless ocean, a vast expanse of absolutely tranquil water in which there is no ripple, no distraction, no current of thought—only a tranquil, calm, mirror-like surface. When this is achieved, we have, on the one hand, ecstasy or mental and physical happiness and well being. On the other hand, we have the mind which is now a worthy instrument capable of seeing into the heart of reality.

VII. WISDOM

IMPORTANCE OF WISDOM

We have come to what is really the crown jewel of the Buddhist tradition of mental development, acknowledged to be the apex of the practice of mental development within all the Buddhist traditions. This is the development of penetrative insight or wisdom (Prajna). There are many statements to the effect that this is the most important element of Buddhist practice. Perhaps one of the best is a statement made by Nagarjuna, a 2nd Century scholar and saint, the founder of the Middle Way School, who said that for the practice of Buddhism, two things are needed—faith and wisdom. Of these, wisdom is the main thing, faith is preliminary.

We can see the importance of wisdom if we look at the various schemes of practice in the Buddhist traditions. For example, in the fundamentals of the Buddhist tradition, in the eight-fold path, wisdom is the third of the three ways of practice (the other two being morality and mental development). Again, in the practice of the Bodhisattva perfections, wisdom is the sixth perfection, and it has a special role to play. In this context, we spoke of wisdom as being like a sighted guide with the help of whose a group of blind men could safely and successfully reach their goal. In the Bodhisattvacaryavatara or Bodhicaryavatara (the Bodhisattva Way of Life), Shantideva said that it was for wisdom's sake that the Buddha taught all the practices that had gone before. So wisdom is the most important component in transforming the experience of an ordinary living being into the enlightened, transformed condition of a Buddha.

Wisdom or insight is not cumulative. It is not the acquisition of knowledge. A Taoist philosopher, Lao-Tzu, said that the student learns by accumulating, the wise learns by discarding. Here too, we are talking about penetrative insight, penetrative wisdom, not accumulation of knowledge, not even mundane wisdom. We are talking about seeing into things, seeing beyond the surface of things.

We can see the very special role that this kind of insight has by looking at the life of the Buddha. In his account of his experiences on the night of his enlightenment, he says that, on that night, with his mind made supple and purified by meditation, he then directed his mind toward the understanding of things as they really are. There are three kinds of knowledge gained by the Buddha on the night of his enlightenment during the three watches of the night, according to the traditional account. During the first watch, the Buddha directed his mind towards the recollection of his former lives. He remembered the circumstances in which he had been born, what his names had been, what his occupations had been, and so forth. In the second watch of the night, he directed his mind towards the knowledge of the working of the law of karma, the law of cause and effect in the lives of all sentient beings, and he was able to see how living beings who are authors of wholesome actions experience fortunate rebirths. While living beings who are authors of unwholesome actions experience unfortunate rebirths. Finally, in the third watch of the night, the Buddha directed his mind towards the understanding of the causes of suffering and rebirth.

This is where he ascertains that the causes of suffering and rebirth are ignorance, desire and ill will. Here we have the imagery of the dawn of the rising sun. Just as the light of wisdom, by means of which the Buddha has understood the causes of suffering and rebirth dawns upon him, so the light of the new day dawns. Here, too, we can see the importance of wisdom, because more than any of the other practices, more than the practice of the perfections of generosity, morality, patience, energy and concentration over countless lifetimes, it is wisdom that turns an unenlightened sentient being into a Buddha. This is why in some Buddhist traditions, such as the Zen tradition, we see so much emphasis on the idea of sudden enlightenment, because when wisdom comes, it is sudden. As one climbs a wall and reaches the top, the moment that one peers over the wall one suddenly sees what lies on the other side. In the same way, when the light of wisdom dawns, there is sudden dawning of the light of knowledge.

In the Buddhist tradition in general, and in the Mahayana tradition in particular, this wisdom is of two types. It is the wisdom of the insubstantiality of the personality (Pudgalanairatmya) and the wisdom of the insubstantiality of phenomena (Dharmanairatmya).

It is important to remember that in Buddhism the development of the wisdom of the insubstantiality of personality and phenomena are pedagogical devices. This can be illustrated with the parable of the raft. In this parable, the Buddha speaks of a man who, finding himself on the bank of a river, makes a raft in order to cross the river. Having reached the other side, if the man were to think that the raft had been very useful to him and to lift the raft up onto his shoulders and proceed on his journey carrying the raft, he would be very foolish. In the same way, the Buddha said that those who find a particular teaching useful in overcoming a particular problem should not cling or hold on to that teaching after it has ceased to become useful. In this way, we have a kind of progressive therapy in Buddhism whereby, in each particular situation, a certain therapy exercises its curative effect, and then is discarded. Another therapy replaces it to cure the next stage of the disorder. It is sometimes said that Buddhism is a tradition that takes away everything, including finally even Buddhism itself. The Zen saying, "If you see the Buddha on the road, kill him," is spoken from the point of view of a transformed nature of being. It means that when you no longer have a headache, you no longer need your aspirin. Similarly, when you become a Buddha you do not need a Buddha. In this context, we will begin with an examination of the insubstantiality of personality, the Buddhist doctrine of not-self (Anatma). This understanding is discarded and replaced with an understanding of the insubstantiality of phenomena, which is also discarded when we are cured and no longer need therapies.

INSUBSTANTIALITY OF PERSONALITY

There are two methods of investigation, which between them reveal the insubstantiality of the personality. The first and better-known method is the analytical method. This proceeds by means of an analysis of personality in terms of the five aggregates, or the live constituents of psychophysical existence (Skandhas—matter, feeling, perception, volition and consciousness). The other method is the relational or synthetic method of investigation which reveals the conditioned and relative nature of the personality.

1 *Analytical Investigation of Personality*

The analytical method involves dissection of what is apparently a unitary and homogeneous entity. This takes place through analyzing the personality into its constituent parts, into the five aggregates. By means of this analytical investigation, one arrives at a view of the personality in which the so-called 'I,' 'the ego,' 'the self,' 'the person,' is just a convenient name for a collection of components in the same way that the term 'forest' is just a convenient name for a collection of trees, or the term 'chariot' is a convenient name for a collection of parts put together in a particular way. Through the process of dissection, we arrive at a view of the personality in which the self is just a convenient name for a collection of mental and physical factors. For example, if the personality were the body, then the personality would be subject to all the transformations that occur to the body. The personality would change along with the body so the body is not the personality. Furthermore, the self or personality does not control the body. If it did so, it would be able to shape the body, direct the body and condition the body according to its will. We all know that we cannot do this. We cannot will our body to be tall or to be short, to be fat or thin. Again, the personality or self is not to be found in the body. There are famous exhaustive analyses of this in Buddhist texts. The hair of the head is not the self, the teeth are not the self, and the mucus and spittle are not the self. Similarly, the body is not in the personality. The personality is not something which is greater or larger than the body, if that were so, we would first have to find the personality, so that we could then say that the body is something that is inside the personality. In these four ways, the self is not to be found in relation to the body—the self is not the body, the self does not possess the body, the self is not found in the body, nor can the body be found in the self.

The same is true of the other aggregates of feeling, perception or idea, volition or habit, and consciousness. The feeling is not the self. The self is not our feeling of pleasure, pain or indifference. The self does not control or possess the feeling. It cannot will happiness, pain or indifference. The self is not to be found in the feeling. The personality is not to be found in any of these aggregates. It does not control any of these aggregates. It is not identical with any of these aggregates. In this way, the self is not to be found in any of these aggregates. It is just a convenient name for a collection of aggregates.

It should be pointed out that we are not denying what we might call the conventional or empirical personality, the personality that appears in everyday language. This is a major confusion. Some people think that Buddhism is denying this conventional 'I'. This is not the case. What Buddhism denies is the notion of a permanent, unchanging personality or self. It may be easy to say that no one could possibly believe in an unchanging self, yet we have all heard people say "That's the way I am, I can't change. This is my nature." These statements are a reflection of the belief in a permanent, unchanging self. This is the self that we are denying here, that is being dissected analytically.

There is a more general way of viewing the five aggregates. The aggregates can be divided into subjective and objective components. Consciousness, volition, perception and feelings are the subjective components in experience (Nama), and matter (Rupa) is the objective component. Our experience may be understood in terms of the subjective component and the objective component. This is not surprising in the light of what we said about the origins of suffering. We said that the sense of self dichotomizes being, existence, experience, into a self and an other than the self. This dichotomy is the basis of desire and aversion. Here, too, in our analysis of experience, we have a self and an other than the self. We have a subject and an object. We have a subjective component which is the mind, together with its habits, ideas and feelings, and we have an objective component which is the physical sense organs (the eyes, the ears, the nose, the tongue, the skin) and the physical, material objects around us.

Thus, we can analyze the personality in terms of subjective and objective components. We can analyze personal experience in terms of subject and object. If we do this, we find that in all our experiences, we have a combination of subjective and objective components. For example, in a visual experience, we have the mind, the eye and the visible object coming together to produce the experience of a visual form. As we look at an object out there, we have a visible object which belongs to the objective component of experience, we have the sense organ, which is material and which also belongs to the objective component of experience, and we have the mind which is the subjective component. These three factors produce visual consciousness. Again, in regard to an audio experience, we have the sound, the sense organ (ear) and the moment of consciousness of sound. The same thing happens with the other senses of smell, taste and so forth.

By dissecting experience into subjective and objective components, we can arrive at a view of experience in which we have, so to speak, isolated the trees from the forest. We no longer experience personality in terms of unitary self, opposed to and in conflict with a unitary object. We then begin to experience personality in terms of objective and subjective components, interacting in processes, changing every moment, acting in combination to produce experience. This is the analytical investigation of personality. It is a dissection of the personality so that we are left with component parts. We are left with a material object, a sense organ and a moment of consciousness. We cease to see the personality in terms of a unitary, unchanging 'I'. Instead we begin to see the personality in terms of impersonal processes.

2 *Relational Investigation of Personality*

We also have a relational, or synthetic, or conditional, investigation of the personality. This investigation demonstrates that the personality exists only in relation to causes and conditions. What are these causes and conditions? Traditionally, there are said to be five— ignorance, craving, clinging, karma and nutrition. Ignorance, craving, clinging and karma are elements which belong to past lives. They belong to the group of afflictions (ignorance, craving, clinging) and to the group of action (karma) which together are the causes of rebirth. Nutrition is an element of this life. The relational causes of personality are the afflictions and karma which belong to the past life, and nutrition which belongs to this life. The personality exists relative to these causes, is dependent upon these causes, conditioned by these causes. By means of these two approaches, we have on the one hand, the analytical investigation of the internal complexity of the personality which reveals that the personality is not a unitary entity, but rather is a collection of parts; and on the other hand, we have the relational investigation which looks at the external relations of the personality, the fact that the personality is dependent upon conditions outside itself. We thus arrive at a conception of the insubstantiality of the personality.

INSUBSTANTIALITY OF PHENOMENA

We have defined wisdom as the understanding of the insubstantiality of personality and the insubstantiality of phenomena. Here, in looking at the insubstantiality of phenomena, we will also be using the two investigative processes, the analytical and the relational methods. Let us look first at phenomena, the objects of our consciousness in the course of our investigation of personality, we have divided personality into objective and subjective components, into objects of consciousness and consciousness itself, into objects of mind and mind itself. Here let us look at the objects in our experience, the objects of which we are aware. We can begin with relatively simple objects around us. We can begin with the table, the chair, the house, the tree.

1 *Analytical Investigation of Phenomena*

In looking at these objects, we can begin again with an analytical investigation. We can look at the parts of the objects. For example, the table before me. We can begin by analyzing, dissecting the table, looking at the parts of the table. In doing so, we will separate the top of the table from the frame, the legs from the crosspieces, etc. We can gradually break down the table into its component parts. In this process of dissecting an object of consciousness, or reducing a material object into its component parts, we eventually arrive at what might be taken to be the smallest constituent part of matter. As we go on with our dissecting of matter, we will eventually arrive at the atom.

The atom was held to be the smallest irreducible component of matter both in India as well as in the West. The Buddhist assailed the unity of an atom. They demonstrated that the atom too was divisible. They did this by means of the following argument. They said that as matter is composed of atoms, the only way that atoms can combine to form an object is by arranging themselves in a particular formation. For atoms to arrange themselves in a particular formation, to collect together, they have to touch. If two or more atoms come together, there will be a near side to the atom, a far side, a top, a bottom, a left and a right to the atom. If the atom has all these parts, then the atom is not indivisible. Even the ostensibly irreducible atom can be further divided. By means of this analytical procedure, they arrive at the notion of the infinite divisibility of atom, which is tantamount to arriving at the infinite divisibility of matter.

2 Relational Investigation of Phenomena

Just as we apply the relational investigation to the personality, we can also apply a relational investigation to objects of consciousness. In this context, objects of consciousness depend on their causes and conditions for their existence. The classical example is the case of the sprout. The sprout does not exist independently. It exists dependent upon the seed, earth, water, air and sunlight. Another classical example is the flame in an oil lamp. The flame exists dependent upon the wick and the oil. So objects of consciousness like the sprout and the flame in an oil lamp depend upon other objects of consciousness for their existence. As we dissect material objects, we find that we can break them up into smaller and smaller parts. But that is not the only way we can investigate them. We can investigate them relationally. We can look at their relation to other objects, their dependence upon other objects. In both these ways, we arrive at the insubstantiality of the objects of consciousness.

RELATIVITY OF PHENOMENA AND CONSCIOUSNESS

There is another very important way that we can arrive at an understanding of the insubstantiality of phenomena. This is made much of in the Mahayana tradition, particularly in the Mind Only school (Cittamatra). According to this school, it is shown how objects of consciousness are wholly dependent upon consciousness for their nature and for their existence.

There are many analogical arguments that are used to demonstrate the fact of the dependence of the objects of consciousness upon consciousness. Perhaps the best of these is the classical analogy of dream. In a dream, it is evident that objects of consciousness appear in the absence of a physical object. All of us, if we examine our own experiences of dreams objectively, will find it exceedingly difficult, if not impossible, to distinguish dream experience from waking experience in any significant or sustainable way. One objection to this is that dream experience can be distinguished from waking experience because dream experience does not produce actual physiological effects. This is refuted by Vasubhandu who points out that dream experience can lead to the emission of semen. Thus, in dreams, physiological effects can take place in the absence of a physical object. There are also other examples. There is the example of the alteration which occurs in the perception of objects when consciousness is influenced by intoxicants or by drugs. Similarly, physical ailments can alter the way in which objects present themselves to consciousness. The white conch shell, for example, appears yellow to someone suffering from jaundice.

Again, the appearance of objects depends upon the karmic propensities, the state of mind of the perceiver. The same object can be a cause of fear for one sentient being and a cause of desire for another sentient being. Classically, Buddhism describes this analysis of the dependence of objects upon consciousness in reference to the experiences of the six realms. It is said that what appears as water to human beings, appears as pus or blood to the hungry ghosts, as molten iron to the hell beings, and as nectar to the gods. The water appears differently to them because of their karmic propensities. But one need not go into the realms of Buddhist cosmology to understand how objects alter their character depending upon their perceiver. For example, a desirable woman is an object of desire to a man, but an object of food to a hungry wolf.

Thus, in all of these cases, objects have no nature of their own. They are relative to the perceiver. The way in which they are experienced depends upon the consciousness, the state of mind of the perceiver. Even their appearance itself is possible wholly within the limits of consciousness as in the example of dreams. These findings which the Buddhist tradition has uncovered, largely as the result of meditative experience, have been substantiated by clinical evidence accumulated in the last few decades. They have been supported by studies of pharmacologically induced altered states of consciousness and confirmed by sensory deprivation experiments where it has been found that subjects who are placed in situations of total sensory deprivation can and often begin to project entire three-dimensional worlds right out of their mind.

To summarize, we have here an investigation of the objects of consciousness. First, we have an analytical investigation in which objects are dissected and reduced to their component parts. Material objects are reduced to their atomic constituents and these atomic constituents are also shown to be divisible. This is followed by a synthetic or relational investigation, in which the dependence of objects on other objects is shown, as in the case of the sprout which is dependent upon the seed, earth, water and so forth. Then, we find that objects are dependent upon consciousness itself. Objects appear dependent upon consciousness. The way in which they appear is also dependent upon consciousness.

Analysis of Consciousness

Thus far, we have an analytical and a relational investigation of objects of consciousness. What about consciousness or mind itself? Is consciousness itself immune to these kinds of analytical and synthetic investigations? If this were the case, the consciousness or mind would become the self, the personality, the substance that we have so far eliminated from the various components of experience. Certainly, consciousness itself is not immune to these investigative methods.

Let us look first at the analytical investigation of consciousness. We find an analytical investigation of consciousness in many texts, especially in the perfection of wisdom texts (Prajnaparamita). In these texts, it is said, "Is mind short or long, is it round or square, is it white or red or blue, is it within or without or in between?" This reveals that it is impossible to put one's finger on mind. Mind is devoid of attributes, it cannot be identified with emotions, habits and ideas. Mind has no definable properties.

Just as we cannot find any mind when we subject it to analytical scrutiny, so too mind is dependent on, or relative to objects of consciousness. If there is no object of consciousness, there is no consciousness which perceives the object. There is no subject apart from an object. Consciousness cannot perceive itself, cannot feel itself. It is said that the tip of a finger cannot feel itself. The blade of a knife cannot cut itself. Consciousness cannot cognize itself. It exists in relation to objects. So we have here an interdependence of consciousness and its object. The object has been shown to be infinitely divisible, to be dependent upon causes and conditions, and to be dependent upon mind itself. Mind itself has been shown to be devoid of any attributes, to be ultimately unfindable, and to be possible only in relation to an object of consciousness. Thus, we can show the insubstantiality, first of personality, and later of the objective and subjective elements of personality.

To summarize, we began our investigation with the personality. We have shown the insubstantiality of the personality by means of analysis and synthesis, by showing that the personality is composed of physical and mental factors and by showing that the personality is dependent upon causes and conditions (the afflictions, karma and nutrition). One can refine this investigation of personality by looking now, in turn, at the component parts of personal experience—the objective content of experience (object) and the subjective content of experience (consciousness). Then one can apply analytical and synthetical investigations to the objects of consciousness, and finally to consciousness itself. In this way, we arrive at the insubstantiality of personality and at the insubstantiality of phenomena.

Why is it that one needs to use both analytical and relational methods of investigation? The fact is, that each of these methods by itself is incomplete. By itself, each of these methods leads to a distorted picture of reality. If one relies wholly on the analytical method, one is left with a static and fragmented view of reality. As one proceeds to break up reality into even smaller and smaller components—material reality into atoms and then into subatomic particles, and mental reality into moments of consciousness—one is left with static bits and pieces of reality. The problem of this view of reality is the problem of explaining the relationship between these bits and pieces. How is it that these fragmented pieces participate in an experience which is dynamic, fluent and integrated? To overcome the limitations of the analytical method, we need to apply the relational method which emphasizes the interdependence of the bits and pieces, that they participate in a dynamic, fluent integrated whole. Only by applying this relational method can we show that these components of experience have no independent existence of their own, that they derive their nature, function, and reality from their participation in a relationship, forming an integrated whole.

In fact, we are here talking about the realistic, pluralistic and absolutist phase of Buddhist philosophy. We are talking about the teaching of the first turning of the wheel of the Dharma in which the aggregates and the elements of experience are taught, and the second turning of the wheel of the Dharma in which the emptiness of all factors of experience is taught.

It is very interesting to see these movements within the Buddhist tradition paralleled in such an uncanny way in the Western scientific tradition. Just as Buddhism uses an analytical approach which is followed by a synthetic approach, Western physics had the mechanistic, reductionist view of Newtonian physics, followed by the holistic, relativistic view of quantum mechanics. A similar thing happened to Western psychology, where the reductionism of the behavioral schools gave rise to the Gestalt schools which emphasize the relativity of psychological phenomena. Right across the entire gamut of Western sciences today, holism and interdependence is gaining importance, balancing the mechanistic and reductionistic views that predominated in the last century.

We also have some parallels in the human brain itself. It has been suggested that the human brain is divided into two hemispheres, and that one hemisphere operates primarily analytically and the other operates primarily intuitively. One hemisphere is good at breaking things up, at being very penetrative. The other half of the brain is better at seeing the whole picture, taking a more holistic view of reality. The person whose analytical half is over-dominant cannot cope with situations that require a holistic view. The person whose intuitive half is over-dominant may not be able to think precisely and cope with analytical tasks. Both the analytical and intuitive faculties are necessary in order to arrive at a balanced view of reality.

EMPTINESS

This balanced view of reality means an understanding of the ultimate truth or the way things really are. This understanding of the insubstantiality both of the personality and of phenomena is referred to as the understanding of emptiness. Emptiness is not nothingness, it is not voidness. It is an English translation of the term Shunyata. Shunyata means emptiness, but it also means fullness, like the fullness of a balloon. Emptiness is the avoidance or the transcendence of the alternatives of existence and non-existence which are basic alternatives in the fabric of human thought. Emptiness is synonymous with inter-dependence. Inter-dependence is existence relative to causes and conditions. Existence that is relative to causes and conditions is neither existence nor non-existence. It is not existence, because conditioned existence comes to an end, it is provisional, dependent, conditional. It is also not non-existence, because it is experienced. It has a conditioned, provisional, relative reality.

Let us look at this in regard to a specific case, such as a sprout. The sprout exists dependent upon the seed, water, etc. It does not exist absolutely, because when the conditions which allow it to exist fail to sustain it, it ceases to exist. So its existence is relative, conditioned and dependent. However, the sprout is not non-existent because it has a provisional existence relative to its causes and conditions. So the emptiness of the sprout means the interdependence of the sprout. It means that the sprout is not absolutely existent and not absolutely non-existent. Similarly, all phenomena, all experience, are beyond existence and non-existence. Every object participates in interdependence. Because they participate in interdependence they are empty. Because they are empty, they are ultimately beyond existence and non-existence.

This emptiness that transcends existence and non-existence has a phenomena quality, an apparitional quality. It has an ability to appear because it is not non-existence. Just as the sprout is not non-existence and has the ability to subsist relative to causes and conditions, so too all phenomena have the ability to appear relative to causes and conditions because they are not ultimately non-existent. This is the phenomenal, or form, dimension of emptiness. This is why it is said in the Heart Sutra that form is emptiness, emptiness is form. Form is not different from emptiness. Emptiness is not different from form. Emptiness is feeling, feeling is emptiness. Emptiness is not different from feeling, feeling is not different from emptiness. The same thing applies to the other aggregates of personal experience—perception, volition and consciousness.

This is the not non-existence of emptiness. Emptiness is beyond existence and non-existence. It transcends existence and non-existence. It is not nothingness. So the positive content of emptiness is its identity, its oneness, its integration with the phenomenal universe of names and forms. The dynamism, the fluidity, lack of fixity, the space in the phenomenal universe is provided by emptiness. This is because phenomena (form, feeling, etc.) are not ultimately existent. Their existence is relative.

THE INTEGRATED VISION

In this particular Buddhist tradition which we are discussing, this idea of the unity of form and emptiness, the unity of phenomena and emptiness, and the going beyond of existence and non-existence is expressed in the idea of the integration of luminosity and emptiness. Just as we might say that form and emptiness are one, so here we say that luminosity and emptiness are one. The integration of luminosity and emptiness is the ultimate vision, the vision that goes beyond existence and non-existence. What does this mean? The emptiness dimension means that all things do not exist in an ultimate unchanging fixed and static way. They are ultimately not existent. That is the emptiness dimension of reality. At the same time, they are not absolutely non-existent because they appear, they manifest themselves. We see them, we feel them, we experience them. We experience all the name and form. They are not non-existence because they are ultimately luminous. They have an ability to appear, to shine so to speak. Thus, the integrated vision is the integration of emptiness and luminosity, openness as opposed to non-existence, fluidity and dynamism as opposed to static reality. This integrated vision, this unity of luminosity and emptiness, is the ultimate truth.

The oneness of luminosity and emptiness also means the oneness of samsara and nirvana. This is one of the very important doctrines of the Mahayana. Nagarjuna, in one of his more famous texts (Mulamadhayamakakarika) says, "There is not the slightest difference between samsara and nirvana—that which is samsara is nirvana, and that which is nirvana is samsara." This is because of the unity of luminosity and emptiness, this unity of form and emptiness. It might be said that form equals samsara, emptiness equals nirvana. Here luminosity equals samsara, emptiness equals nirvana. Reality is integrated, non-dual, undivided. It has a luminous aspect which is samsara, and it has an empty aspect which is nirvana.

At this stage, as we reach the highest level in our progress towards the pure vision, what has happened to the experience of suffering? After all, the Buddhist tradition begins with the experience of suffering. As we break the notion of the duality of self and an other than the self with the understanding of the insubstantiality of personality and phenomena, we transform samsara, the experience of suffering, not by eliminating it, not by turning it into nothing, but by purifying it. What used to be an impure experience, what used to be suffering, now becomes the experience of luminosity, that inconceivable spontaneous activity of the enlightened beings. Enlightenment or nirvana here does not mean nothingness. It does not mean becoming absorbed or immersed, disappearing into emptiness. It means becoming one with ultimate reality, which has a luminous dimension as well as an empty dimension. This luminous dimension, on the stage of enlightenment, becomes a positive vibrant energy which can take all kinds of forms, in order to help to liberate other sentient beings.

This is where we begin to talk of the soteriological activities of the Bodhisattvas, wherein the Bodhisattvas take on all forms and shapes, including the forms of the Tantric deities of the Vajrayana pantheon. On the stage of enlightenment, this luminosity manifests itself in the various soteriological devices, in the various deities, in the various activities of the Bodhisattvas, who, like the whole of the universe, are not non-existent. But, they are also not existent in a fixed, limited, stultified way. They have this fluid, dynamic, empty, open quality.

NON-ABIDING NIRVANA

This unity of luminosity and emptiness, of samsara and nirvana is reflected in the goal of the Mahayana tradition, the non-abiding nirvana which is not fixed, which does not dwell either in samsara, or in nirvana. Herein, the enlightened Bodhisattvas, because of their compassion, do not dwell in nirvana. They do not dwell in emptiness. They make use of this luminous dimension of samsara to perform inconceivable activities for the benefit of living beings. At the same time, because of their wisdom, because of their understanding of the insubstantiality of personality and of phenomena, they are not bound in samsara. They are free. Their freedom has a kind of amphibious quality wherein they can move freely between this empty dimension and this luminous dimension, Of course, when we use the language of movement, we are using a metaphor taken from our own experience. In the case of the enlightened ones, there is no movement from one dimension to another. Within their own being, there is an integration, a unity of these two dimensions of luminosity and emptiness which are non-dual, which are interpenetrating.

Herein, we have the conception of the two dimensions of Buddhahood—the form dimension (Rupakaya) and the inconceivable, transcendental dimension (Dharmakaya). The luminous dimension of ultimate reality is mirrored in the form dimension of Buddhahood, and the empty dimension of ultimate reality is mirrored in the transcendental dimension of Buddhahood.

This ends our discussion of the experience of transformation, of the experience of the yogin who awakens the thought of enlightenment and who sets out on the Bodhisattva path which will bring him to the threshold of Buddhahood. We will next look at the fruit of the tradition of mental development, the state of Buddhahood.

VIII. ENLIGHTENMENT AND BUDDHAHOOD

THE THREE EXPERIENCES

On a few occasions, I have referred to the idea of the three experiences or the Triple Vision. In fact, most of the material and the entire framework that I have made use of has been adopted from a body of teaching called the Triple Vision. This body of teaching was first transmitted as an oral tradition from India to Tibet between the 7th and 13th Centuries. Later, it was written down in various versions in Tibet. The Triple Vision teaching not only provides a practical guide to the meditational practices of the Mahayana, it also serves as an introduction to the Tantric phase of Buddhist practice (Vajrayana). It has been used to fulfil this two-fold purpose throughout the history of the Tibetan Buddhist tradition.

The three experiences are the impure experience, the experience of transformation, and the pure experience. The impure experience refers to the illusory vision and the karmic vision—the illusory vision which is the experience that is engendered by the illusion of self and by the emotive instability that results from the illusion of self; and the karmic vision which is the experience that sentient beings have as a result of the wholesome and unwholesome actions that they have performed impelled by ignorance, attachment and aversion. To put it simply, the impure experience is the experience of the six realms of samsara. What is common in these six realms is suffering in its particular manifestations of birth, old age, sickness, death, separation from loved ones, proximity to those whom we dislike, and the destitution of desired objects. Suffering in all these particular manifestations is endemic in all the six realms of existence.

This impure experience begins to give way to the experience of transformation through a positive transformational practice so that at the level of impure experience, our main object is to get away from impure experience, which is a negative process of disengagement. On the stage of experience of transformation, we have a positive kind of engagement. This process takes place through the cultivation of universal love and compassion, the awakening of the enlightenment thought and the practices of the six perfections of the Bodhisattva path, particularly the practice of tranquility and insight. This in turn gives way to the pure transformed experience on the stage of fruition.

We can see these three experiences as constituting the cause, the path and the fruit of the process of mental development. We can see the impure experience as the cause. It is because of the experience of suffering in the six realms that we have the cause of embarking on a program of mental development. This is in part why Buddhism never felt it necessary to be a particularly proselytizing religion because there is always a tacit acceptance of the fact that suffering would in itself be the factor that would precipitate interest in taking up a discipline of self-development. The transformational experience functions as the process of the transformation. The fruit of this process is the transformed pure experience which is Buddhahood.

THE PURE EXPERIENCE

The purpose of considering the pure experience of Buddhahood is to derive a certain inspiration and confidence about the goal for which we are striving. Just as when a man in a desert upon hearing of an oasis would be inspired and refreshed, so one may likewise upon hearing about the fruit of this path of self-development be inspired and refreshed. Similarly, one will be more inclined to undertake the difficulties of making the necessary arrangements when one is shown a photograph of the place that one intends to spend the holiday.

Arriving at the pure experience means arriving at the experience of ultimate reality. This experience is of course distinguished from the experience of conventional or apparent reality. The experience of ultimate reality entails not grasping, not relinquishing and not abiding in any phenomena, object or idea (dharma). Because it means not grasping any dharma, it also means not relinquishing any dharma. Since the dharma are not grasped in the first place, there is no need to relinquish them. Similarly, there is no abiding in the dharma, no becoming fixed in them. Phenomena, objects and ideas are like little compartments that we shut ourselves in. So long as we shut ourselves up in these little compartments, there will be no growth.

Perhaps we can understand this better if we again have recourse to some analogical comparisons. You may recall the anecdote of the dream of the virgin girl. Similarly, it is said that this whole world is like an illusory elephant that is created by the art of magic. Another example is the holograph. The holograph can create a three-dimensional image of an object. You can look around the object but there is no object. It is created by beams of light. All phenomena are like a dream, a magical illusion, or a holograph. They appear relative to causes and conditions. They have no ultimate reality. The birth, the continuation and the death of all objects and ideas are like the origin, the duration and the destruction of an object in a dream, conjured by a magical illusion or created by a holograph. They are simply existences that appear relative to causes and conditions. They are all apparitional existences. The conclusion that is to be drawn from this is that birth and death have no ultimate reality. Birth and death are an occasion for suffering so long as one remains in the dream state. On the level of enlightenment, birth and death ceased to be an occasion for suffering because they are now understood to be the birth and death of objects seen in a dream. In the same way that one might awaken from a dream, on the enlightenment stage one awakens from the illusion of birth and death.

BUDDHA-NATURE

In explaining the pure experience, the Mahayana tradition of mental development often has recourse to the idea of the Buddha-nature, the potentiality within each and every one of us to achieve Buddhahood. Buddha-nature is a loose translation of the term Tathagatagarbha, which actually means the womb, the place of birth of Buddhahood. What is this Buddha-nature which is often spoken of in many Mahayana texts, especially in the Mind Only tradition? The Buddha-nature is the nature of the mind as the integrated state of luminosity and emptiness. We spoke about the ultimate reality as being the integration of luminosity and emptiness. We liken this combination of luminosity and emptiness to the identity of form and emptiness that we find in the Heart Sutra. We also liken this to the unity of samsara and nirvana.

Let us look at some practical examples in order to understand what we mean by the Buddha-nature being equivalent to the clear and empty nature of mind. The mind may be likened to a crystal. The crystal has the potential to reflect any one of a number of colors and yet it has no color of its own. This can be said to be the luminosity and the emptiness of crystal: the luminosity is the potential to reflect a variety of colors and the emptiness is the nature of the crystal in having no color of its own. For example, if we place the crystal before a red background, the crystal will appear red. The mind is similar to the crystal in that it too has the capacity to yield a number of experiences, and that is its luminosity, and at the same time it has no definite mode of existence of its own, and that is its emptiness. If we expose the mind to the afflictions, the mind will yield the experience of suffering, the impure experience. Conversely, if we expose the mind to the transforming experience, to non-ignorance, non-attachment and non-aversion, the mind will yield the pure experience, the experience of Buddhahood. Like a crystal, the mind has a luminous nature and yet has no nature of its own. Similarly, a white cloth has the potential to have any one of a number of colors and yet it has no color of its own. If we dye the cloth red for instance, it will become red.

There is a story told by a great and living Tibetan master that illustrates nicely this idea of Buddha-nature. He said that suppose we have a lump of brass and we fashion this lump of brass into a chamber pot. We use the chamber pot for keeping excrement and urine and everyone will consider it filthy and impure and will despise the pot. Suppose we melt down the chamber pot and fashion it into a vessel of offering. The vessel will be used for offering at the shrine. Suppose we take this offering vessel and melt it down into an image of the Buddha. It will be an object of veneration. Throughout the whole process, the lump of brass has been the same. It has the potential to yield up all different forms and yet it has no form of its own. We can complete this analogy by likening the chamber pot to unenlightened sentient beings who have not embarked upon any discipline of mental development. Such a being is buried in the impure experience, and he is looked down upon by everyone around him. If we expose him to the experience of transformation, he becomes like that offering vessel. He becomes a means of approaching enlightenment and Buddhahood. Finally, through the elimination of ignorance, attachment and aversion, he becomes an object of worship. This is the Buddha-nature, the combination of potential and emptiness that is the actual nature of our mind. Through the presence of certain conditions, it can yield up Buddhahood although through the presence of other conditions it yields up the impure vision, the experience of samsara.

DEFINITION OF BUDDHAHOOD

Let us look at the actual nature of the fruit of mental development. The term Buddha, which is often translated as 'the enlightened one' or 'the awakened one' means one who has achieved freedom from the afflictions—ignorance, desire and ill will—and also one who has acquired countless positive qualities, who has, as some put it, completely evolved. Let us look at the Tibetan translation of this term

Buddha because it will help to shed some light on the meaning of Buddhahood. The Tibetan translation is 'Sang Gye'. This word actually consists of two terms 'Sang' which means purified and 'Gye' which means expanded or extended. This indicates clearly the two-fold character of Buddhahood. On the one hand it means the purification of the afflictions of ignorance, desire and ill will, and on the other hand it means extension or evolvement.

A Buddha is one who has through the practice of the six perfections achieved the two accomplishments—the accomplishment of merit and the accomplishment of knowledge and who has gained the three dimensions or bodies (kayas) of Buddhahood—the Dharmakaya (truth dimension), the Sambhogakaya (celestial dimension) and the Nirmanakaya (terrestrial dimension). These three dimensions may be subsumed into two dimensions—the Dharmakaya and the Rupakaya (phenomenal dimension which includes the celestial and terrestrial dimensions). These two dimensions correspond to the two accomplishments. The accomplishment of merit leads to the realization of the Rupakaya, and the accomplishment of knowledge leads to the realization of the Dharmakaya.

These two dimensions which follow from the accomplishment of merit and knowledge fulfill a two-fold purpose. For Buddhism, the object is always to benefit oneself and others. We are not teaching a tradition of self-sacrifice. We are dealing with the tradition that always strive for both the self and others. This is reflected in these two dimensions of Buddhahood. The Rupakaya is for the benefit of others, to help others to achieve Buddhahood. The Dharmakaya is for one's own benefit. This is also a reflection of the idea of freedom from and freedom to. The

Rupakaya is an expression of the Buddha's freedom to engage in the activities of the world in order to help other sentient beings. The Dharmakaya is an expression of the Buddha's freedom from, an expression of his transcendence of the world.

ATTRIBUTES OF THE BUDDHA

Traditionally, a lot of time is spent on describing the attributes of the Buddha. The attributes are classified under five headings—body, voice, mind, qualities and activities. You will notice that there is a certain amount of overlapping between the classifications which is inevitable, and also a certain degree of artificiality. Nonetheless, this scheme of classification serves as a useful scheme for categorizing and enumerating some of the more important qualities of Buddhahood.

1 *Body of the Buddha*

In regard to the body of the Buddha, we have first to remember all that was said regarding the Buddha's possession of the three bodies—the Dharmakaya, the Sambhogakaya and the Nirmanakaya, and the nature of the three bodies. Besides this, it is repeatedly stated that the body of the Buddha is infinitely diverse, inconceivably vast and all encompassing. We have a suggestion of what has sometimes been called the pantheon of the Mahayana because in the final analysis, on the stage of the pure experience, the whole universe may be seen as an expression of the principle of enlightenment that we personify as the Buddha. We are now breathing a somewhat different atmosphere because when we talk about the Buddha, we no longer have in mind the figure of the historical Buddha Sakyamuni who lived and taught in India. In the context of the three dimensions of Buddhahood, the diverse, inconceivable, vast and all-encompassing being of the Buddha, the Buddha Sakyamuni is just one (be it a special one) manifestation of Buddhahood.

2 *Voice of the Buddha*

The voice of the Buddha is endowed with incomparable qualities. Among the more interesting qualities is the ability to reply to many questions simultaneously, the ability to express himself in many languages of the hearer simultaneously, and the ability to hear at diverse distances. In particular, in regard to this second attribute, the many arguments over the language with which the Buddha taught pale into insignificance because the Buddha taught in the language of his interlocutor. Each of them heard him in the language that was intelligible to them.

3 *Mind of the Buddha*

The mind of the Buddha is perhaps the most exalted of all the attributes of Buddhahood. In the briefest explanation, it is said to have two qualities of knowledge—the knowledge of all things as they are believed to be and the knowledge of all things as they are. This corresponds to the two levels of reality—the conventional level and the ultimate level of reality. The knowledge of the Buddha has to encompass these two levels because it is the purpose and function of the Buddha to build a bridge, so to speak, between the conventional reality and the ultimate reality. How else could the Buddha lead sentient beings to freedom without mastery of the conventional truth with which sentient beings are all conversant, and the ultimate reality which is the peculiar fruit of enlightenment, the special acquisition of the Buddha.

In addition to this two-fold description, there is the four-fold description of the mind of the Buddha. According to this description, the mind of the Buddha is endowed with four kinds of transcendental knowledge. The first is the mirror-like knowledge. This is a variety of knowledge which reflects the actual essence of all phenomena. This is analogous to the knowledge of the ultimate reality in the two-fold description.

The second knowledge is the knowledge of equanimity. This entails the attitude of equanimity towards samsara or nirvana. The Buddha is not inclined to either samsara and nirvana. This corresponds to the so-called non-abiding nirvana of the Buddha which does not allow him to settle down either in samsara or in nirvana. This knowledge of equanimity too is indispensable for the saving work of the Buddha because if the Buddha were inclined to nirvana, there would be a withdrawal from samsara and the saving function would be impaired.

The third knowledge is the knowledge of discrimination. Whereas the first knowledge is the mirror-like knowledge which implies the sameness of all things, the discriminating knowledge is the knowledge of all things as they appear to different sentient beings in their various particular situations.

The fourth knowledge is the knowledge of accomplishments. Whereas the knowledge of discrimination is the knowledge of things in their particular variegated forms, the knowledge of accomplishment is the knowledge of disposition and attitude of sentient beings.

You can see how all these four kinds of knowledge work together to contribute to the saving work engaged in by the Buddha. The knowledge of all things as they are is tantamount to his proper knowledge of ultimate reality. The knowledge of equanimity causes him not to settle down in nirvana and therefore to function freely in the world of samsara. The discriminating knowledge enables him to know the particular modes of all objects. The accomplishing knowledge enables him to know the particular dispositions of sentient beings so that he can best help them to achieve enlightenment.

4 Qualities of the Buddha

Generally, the numerous qualities of the Buddha fall into two categories. The first category consists of the special, apparent qualities of the Buddha. These are the thirty-two major and eighty minor marks of a great person. The thirty-two marks include the protuberance at the top of the head and the circle of hair between the eyebrows. They are also the marks that adorn the physical form of the historical Buddhas and the celestial Buddhas. The second category consists of the qualities possessed solely by the Buddha—the eighteen Buddha Dharma, and this includes the quality of never making nonsensical utterances and having an unfailing memory. These are the special marks that adorn the physical form and the special properties that adorn the character of the Buddha.

5 Activities of the Buddha

The special activities of the Buddha are characterized by spontaneity. What we have here is the activities of all the phenomenal manifestations of Buddhahood that belong either to the terrestrial dimension or to the celestial dimension. All these activities that are undertaken for the benefit of all sentient beings are undertaken not in a premeditated way. This has to be seen in the Buddha's oneness with ultimate reality because in ultimate reality where there is no distinction between samsara and nirvana, between unenlightened beings and enlightened beings, there cannot be a premeditated, deliberate action. This is the inconceivable, unthinkable activities of the Buddha, the spontaneous activities through the medium of the different particular expressions of the terrestrial and celestial dimensions. Through this medium, the Buddha undertakes diverse and countless inconceivable activities for the liberation of sentient beings.

One modern writer has likened these activities to placing a plane on auto-pilot. Having created the momentum for that phenomenal manifestation through the Buddha's practice of the perfections, the Buddha no longer needs to direct his activities in a premeditated and deliberate way. The phenomenal dimension which is born of the Buddha's practice of the perfections leading to the accomplishment of merit acts on its own. It is, so to speak, pre-programmed to accomplish the benefit of sentient beings.

There are a couple of classical examples of the inconceivable activities of the Buddha for the benefit of sentient beings. Traditionally, it is said that this spontaneous activity is like the setting up of a pillar which has the ability to cure poison. In ancient India and even today, persons who have special ability to neutralize the poison of venomous snakes are sought after. Just as one of these healers would occasionally set up a pillar or leave behind an object which has the ability to purify the poison even long after the healer has moved on, in the same way, the Buddha, through his practice of the perfections, sets up phenomenal appearances—entities, objects, persons, in space and time, which have the power to liberate sentient beings. The Buddha himself does not any longer need to engage in a premeditated and deliberate way in his saving activities. This spontaneous activity is also likened to the operation of a wind chime which responds automatically to the currents of air that strike against it, giving off louder or softer sounds.

PHENOMENAL DIMENSION OF BUDDHAHOOD

1 *Sambhogakaya*

The vehicle for these activities of the Buddha is the phenomenal dimension of Buddhahood— the Sambhogakaya and the Nirmanakaya. The Sambhogakaya, which is loosely translated here as the celestial dimension, literally means the body, being or existence of bliss, enjoyment or refulgence. Actually, this dimension of Buddhahood refers to a very special, exalted dimension of Buddhahood. It is not a form of Buddhahood that is accessible to all. It is only accessible to sentient beings whose vision has been purified. This is why the Sambhogakaya is called the divine dimension of Buddhahood. Buddhas and Bodhisattvas of this dimension are the Buddhas of the five families (Buddhas Vairocana, Ratnasambhava, Amitabha, Amoghasiddhi, Akshobhya) and the heavenly Bodhisattvas Avalokiteshvara, Maitreya, Manjushri, etc. These figures do not belong to the earthly dimension. To those whose vision has not been purified, they are accessible only as figures in art. They are not available as objects in direct experience. But to the meditators who have purified their vision, these celestial

Buddhas and Bodhisattvas appear directly. The special function of the Sambhogakaya is the teaching of the Mahayana. They engage exclusively in the teachings of the Mahayana.

2 Nirmanakaya

The term Nirmanakaya is here loosely translated as the terrestrial dimension. Nirmana means created, emanated, produced. Nirmanakaya is a produced body, a fabricated body. The Nirmanakaya appears on the earthly plane even to those whose vision has not been purified. The most important and special appearance of the Nirmanakaya was the historical Buddha Sakyamuni. In addition to this specially created appearance in the form of the Buddha Sakyamuni who enacts the drama of renunciation of the household life, the quest for enlightenment, the enlightenment under the Bodhi tree and then teaches the Dharma to the world, there are other Nirmanakayas. These are of two kinds—the incarnate appearances in the form of friends of virtue, and the created magical appearances in the form of visions and inanimate objects. The incarnate appearances allow for the emanations of Buddhahood in the realms of the gods and even amongst human beings. They are the created forms which are born. For example, in the Tibetan tradition, there is the institution of recognized Nirmanakayas—Tulkus (which literally means Nirmanakaya) and Rinpoches (precious ones). These spiritual friends and teachers who live and teach among human beings are recognized to be the Nirmanakayas of the Buddha. This is one way that the Buddha's phenomenal dimension appears and functions in the world and that is through taking birth in human forms.

The Nirmanakaya can also appear simply as magical creations. These can be in the form of persons, as for example, the vision with which the Buddha created to convert Queen Kshema; or in the form of inanimate objects. When Shantideva, in his Bodhisattvacaryavatara, outlines his aspiration to perform the activities of an exalted Bodhisattva, he says, "May I become food for the hungry, clothing for those without it, shelter for the homeless and medicine for the sick."

The relationship between the Sambhogakaya and Nirmanakaya is made clearer in the Tibetan tradition. Presently, one of the best known of the phenomenal dimensions is the figure of the Dalai Lama. The Dalai Lama is the terrestrial dimension of the Bodhisattva Avalokiteshvara. Whereas the Bodhisattva Avalokiteshvara is not directly accessible to all of us, the Dalai Lama represents the immediate accessibility of Buddhahood at the level of ordinary sentient beings. Another example is the Sakya Trizin. He is the terrestrial dimension of the exalted Bodhisattva Manjushri.

TRANSFORMATIONS OF FORMS, SOUNDS AND THOUGHTS

We have talked about the experience of the Buddha in terms of his identification with ultimate reality, in terms of the transcendence of birth and death, in terms of their unreality. At this stage, let us look at the more positive contents of the pure experience of Buddhahood, of what it might actually be like to experience the pure vision. The transformation which is implied by the appropriation of the pure experience entails the transformation of forms which belong to the sphere of bodily or physical experience, the transformation of sounds which belong to the sphere of verbal experience, and the transformation of thoughts which belong to the sphere of mental experience.

I have said that on the level of the spiritually advanced, one then has direct access to the divine Buddhas and Bodhisattvas. The fruit of the process of mental development is the experience of forms as the forms of the celestial Buddhas and Bodhisattvas, and as the forms of the environment in which the celestial Buddhas and Bodhisattvas dwell. The transformation of experience in terms of forms means that one begins to experience in terms of the celestial Buddhas and Bodhisattvas and in terms of the habitat of the celestial Buddhas and Bodhisattvas. In practical terms, this means that on the level of the purified experience, we begin to experience ourselves as the celestial Buddhas and Bodhisattvas and those around us as other enlightened beings inhabiting these heavenly fields.

We begin to experience sound as the sound of celestial sutras and mantras. We begin to experience sound as transformed divine sound that is the verbal component in the experience of the divine universe. Once when I asked a Tibetan master whether he found it difficult to live in the city because of the noise, he replied that he did not find it at all difficult because the noise of the city was to be perceived as the celestial sound of sutras and mantras.

Finally, mental activities are to be regarded as the inconceivable transcendental dimension of Buddhahood (Dharmakaya).

This purified vision which is characteristic of the experience of Buddhahood is also definitive of the Vajrayana. If we are to look at the quintessentials of the three major Buddhist traditions – Theravada, Mahayana and Vajrayana, we would have to summarize them as follows. The essence of the attitude of the Theravada tradition is to avoid harming other sentient beings. The essence of the attitude of the Mahayana tradition is to seek to benefit other sentient beings. The essence of the attitude of the Vajrayana is to regard oneself and sentient beings as enlightened beings inhabiting the celestial purified universe, and the sounds and shapes around us as the sounds and shapes of the celestial purified universe.

THE THREE STAGES OF PRACTICE

In conclusion, I would like to refer briefly to two points. The first is the three stages of practice—the preliminary practice, the actual practice and the concluding practice. In fact, this material is intended to be made the subject matter of meditation. We utilize the three-stage scheme of practice, beginning with the taking of refuge and the creation of the enlightenment thought, followed by the contemplation of the contents of each of the sessions, whether it be the contemplation of the suffering of the six realms, impermanence and the opportune nature of the human situation, universal love and compassion, etc. All these constitute the actual practice. This is followed by the practice of dedicating the merit from this practice to the enlightenment of all sentient beings. If one keeps this three-stage scheme for practice in mind, one can slot any part of the contents of these sessions into any meditative practice.

MEDITATIONAL RETREATS

The practice of meditative retreat is the practice of creating a degree of isolation of body, voice and mind wherein one deliberately constricts oneself to a restricted sphere of physical activity and devotes oneself for a varying amount of time each day to the practice of meditation. Depending on one's capacity, one can spend as much as twelve hours or as little as five hours on meditation each day. Ordinarily, these periods of meditation are distributed over three to four sessions so that one might perhaps undertake one session each in the morning, in the afternoon, in the evening and later at night. Each session may last from two to four hours. In this way, one can bring to bear on the meditative process sufficient time and endeavor to make some headway. No doubt tension and frustration will arise. But the meditative experience in a retreat situation is particularly potent.

I would like to end with a remark that the Dalai Lama made a few years ago. He said that whenever we encounter new teachings, we may find them either immediately useful to us, or we may find that we cannot make any use of them, because we may have reservations about the teachings, or because they do not make any sense to us. This may be illustrated by the case of a person who goes to a shop and who sees a lamp which is attractive to him. He buys that lamp, but when he gets home, he finds that the lamp does not fit into the decor of his house. What would you do if you were in this kind of situation? You could either throw away the lamp, or you could put it in the closet with the idea that at a later time you might find a place for it. In the same way with new teachings, rather than rejecting the teachings, just put it aside and sometime later you may find some use for them in your life.

Manjushri Press began as Prajna Press in India where it published important Buddhist texts in Tibetan. It has since been reorganized as Manjushri Press and now publishes books in English about Buddhism and Tibet. For more information about our projects, please contact:

Manjushri Press
P.O. Box 391042
Cambridge, Massachusetts 02139
USA
phone/fax: (617) 492-2614
e-mail: MANJUSHRI@earthlink.net